ART
IN HUMAN AFFAIRS

ART
IN HUMAN AFFAIRS

An Introduction to the Psychology

of Art

by Norman Charles Meier, Ph.D.

Associate Professor of Social and Art Psychology
University of Iowa

FIRST EDITION

McGRAW-HILL BOOK COMPANY, INC.

NEW YORK AND LONDON

1942

ART IN HUMAN AFFAIRS

COPYRIGHT, 1942, BY THE
McGRAW-HILL BOOK COMPANY, INC.

PRINTED IN THE UNITED STATES OF AMERICA

THE MAPLE PRESS COMPANY, YORK, PA.

PREFACE

This volume was prepared with two purposes in mind: first, to set forth a viewpoint holding that art has too long been regarded in a narrow and limited perspective, as though it embraced chiefly those products of man now reposing in museums or visible in his edifices; and, second, to present a consistent and simplified view of the nature of art, its creation, and its significance in the affairs of man, based partly upon a decade of research and partly upon the author's own study from his special vantage point of social and art psychologist and 'occasional' painter.

To accomplish these objectives the author took into consideration findings of cultural anthropology, ethnology, sociology, economic history, social institutions, social psychology, art psychology, archaeology, aesthetics, and art education. Although no one will expect more than a fair acquaintance with some of these fields of knowledge, such contacts are essential to the attainment of that world and time perspective through which alone the real function of art in the life of man may be envisaged at all. Fine distinctions between what is art and what is not art are not even entertained. Comparative evaluations are not made. Datings are of little concern, and Great Periods have no more attention than remote or recent developments.

The primary concern in this volume is to see art not as a thing apart, but as an activity integral with the development of man's cultural existence. Not only is it possible to view art itself in a long-range time perspective, through which its nature and significance gradually emerge in understandable fashion, but the perplexing related problems of special ability, creative imagination, and the interlinking of heredity and environment also become part and parcel of a consistent, unified, and logical whole. No one will, it is hoped, assume that the viewpoint is either wholly correct or incorrect: time alone will be the final corrective, and the whole, complete truth perhaps never known, but the viewpoint set down herein is at least not inconsistent with extant knowledge.

As a phase of the process of rendering the field more consistent throughout, modern art is treated as *experimental* art; as products of trial and error, of introducing variations, of consolidating technical advances, of groping attempts to discover new means altogether. These efforts are assumed to be sincere and an attempt is made to evaluate them objectively. Regarding modern art as experimental art permits, furthermore, avoidance of the time-sequence error, namely, that the latest is necessarily the most advanced in quality. Progression in art is not irreversible: mere passage of time does not in itself confer additive increments of value. All that is certain is that there is change, following periods of increasing or decreasing interest and activity: the ensuing art production may be superior, indifferent, or inferior. In the position taken here, 'modern' is an indefinite designation, evaluation of any product being determined by more significant and permanent considerations.

The treatment of special ability and creative processes constitutes a relatively new position, an outcome of extensive research, special case studies, contacts with producing artists, and checking with data in related fields. The presentation here is merely a sketch of the complete picture, since the detailed, factual material is published in fairly complete form in scientific journals, to which the reader desiring the more explicit account is referred. The material may contribute, it is hoped, toward eventual removal of the unwarranted halo of mystery surrounding the artist's creative processes. The inter-linkage theory of special ability offers a constructive analysis of the concepts of talent, aptitude, and genius in the field of art, indicating concretely the involved interlinking of heredi-tary, environmental, and developmental factors. This view, with its contribution to the tangled nature-nurture problem, is in harmony with accepted views of genetics and biology, as well as being consistent with the assembled data from artists, special studies of children, and other data derived in the research program Genetic Studies in Artistic Capacity, directed by the author from 1929 to 1939.

In the last chapter there are outlined some of the concrete ways in which art is affecting current affairs, and in the appendix there are presented brief notes on fifteen of the pro-ducing artists with whom the author enjoyed contact. In this material are included not only pertinent items concerning heredity and development, but also their philosophies of art, and indications of creative procedures.

In the preparation of this volume the author is greatly indebted for the material aid rendered by the Carnegie Foundation for the Advancement of Teaching and to Dr. Frederick Keppel of the Carnegie Corporation for his interest and series of grants, making possible the research in the genetic aspects of artistic aptitude and the inclusion of the color plates. The Spelman Foundation also contributed a share of the funds permitting the investigation of the beginnings of aesthetic interest and expression of art activities in preschool and later ages in children. Likewise, the author enjoyed the able cooperation of twenty research assistants, who, working under his direction, carried on the major portion of the original studies. These individuals, trained in art, in art education, child art, and social psychology, brought to bear upon the problems a wealth of complementary and supplementary approaches that surmounted limitations of the usual isolated and piecemeal approaches. To the thousands of school children and adults who served as subjects and the school officials who permitted the use of their schools in various cities and smaller communities over ten years, the author likewise owes a debt of gratitude. Finally, about fifty nationally known artists, in discussions with the author, provided that necessary check and corrective to the direction and orientation needed in carrying out the entire research program.

Of the contributions of many others in scattered places, who by correspondence or direct contact added something to the ideas here set forth, the author is deeply appreciative.

In a sense these viewpoints as set forth are minimal statements. This was purposely done to save the reader's time and to make the perspective more comprehensive and the nature of art more comprehensible. The book could have been several times this size but has been intentionally restricted to outline form, leaving to the interested reader amplified presentations of data to be found in the published articles of the author and his coworkers in scientific and other journals. To these, thirty of which appear in issues of the *Psychological Monographs* of 1933, 1936, and 1939, frequent reference is made in footnotes and in the text. The author expresses appreciation to the Psychological Review Publishing Company for permitting the use of certain summary material and illustrations previously appearing in the monographs. The reader will also find in the bibliographies at the end of each chapter other source materials which constitute specific or general bases for the viewpoints developed in the volume. Acknowledgment for the use of illustrative material appears also at the place where the material is used. The author's appreciation is also expressed to his secretary, Marjorie Anderson Synhorst, for her many critical comments and aid in the preparation of the manuscript.

Iowa City, Iowa,
January, 1942.

NORMAN CHARLES MEIER.

CONTENTS

Chapter III

EXPERIMENTAL (MODERN) ART

Chapter IV

CREATIVE PRODUCTION AND ARTISTIC TALENT

Chapter V

ART IN CONTEMPORARY HUMAN AFFAIRS

APPENDIX

ART

IN HUMAN AFFAIRS

An Introduction to the
Psychology of Art

Chapter 1 · THE FUNCTIONS OF ART IN HUMAN EXPERIENCE

1. ART AND LIFE

Man has been prone generally to undervalue art in its relation to human welfare. This lack of appreciation, coming from an inability to attain a proper perspective, is readily understandable: few individuals have opportunity to observe art's multiform nature, its varied functions, and its full imprint on the daily life of peoples everywhere. Only the alert world traveler or the professional student of culture covering widely scattered regions are so favored, and even they may but begin to envisage its full nature and comprehend its varied functions. We cannot all be anthropologists or curators of art in museums or fieldworkers in archaeological investigations; but we may arrive at a better estimate of the service that art has rendered to the advancement of civilization by examining material and findings now available and by giving this rich heritage a psychological interpretation with aid from many quarters. By maintaining an open-minded attitude of inquiry, by attempting to understand the artifacts left by extinct peoples, by approaching sympathetically the mental outlook of members of primitive societies, and by interrelating recurrent phenomena present at all stages of development, we may attain some comprehension of the more significant and fundamental

3

aspects of the important role that art has played in the life of mankind.

When a proper perspective has been reached it becomes indeed very strange that art should be so inadequately evaluated. But again this may be easily explained in a somewhat different manner. In addition to lack of opportunity for contact, conditions present in modern social organization have worked against understanding. The complexity and fast tempo of modern civilization have, in fact, tended to *prevent* an understanding of art. Preoccupation with insistent and seemingly unending demands in earning a living and providing primary comforts has crowded out nearly all avenues of contact with art, leaving many without much hope of ever comprehending it. In that dilemma the usual outcome has been a separation of the two—a regarding of art as a mysterious and esoteric experience to be indulged in when occasion afforded. Visiting an art gallery, attending a lecture, witnessing a drama, or auditing a recital have come to be infrequent, almost awesome experiences associated vaguely with the 'nobler' aspirations. The more the separation has become manifest, the more difficult it has become for the individual to obtain a proper perspective. Dealers in art objects have probably not contributed greatly in efforts to dispel the atmosphere of mystery. Even those who work directly with art have been at times confused, inadequately comprehending its past and feeling uncertain regarding its present and future.

Looking back over the long perspective of human development the present-day attitude seems altogether unnecessary—indeed, unfortunate!

Art in its broad sense did not appear suddenly in the world. Art emerged with man.[1] It served him in ways that are as yet but dimly perceived.

---

[1] Perhaps more exact is Orozco's statement that art may be likened to a stream, "from an unknown beginning to an unknown end." Dickerson, *The Orozco Frescoes at Dartmouth*. Hanover, N. H.: 1934, Introduction.

Far from being turned to as a 'nobler' interest, art has been a part of his daily living—even aiding him in his struggle for existence. With primitive man the arrow that went straight to its mark was symmetrical and balanced—as aestheticians might now describe it—but to him it was an object good to look upon. Objects in nature and those of his own creation that were satisfying to contemplate *were those of good form.* As man progressed through the ages, developing in intelligence, developing in religious conceptions, and improving his technical proficiency, he likewise enlarged his capacity to create and enjoy. This expansion, furthermore, was paralleled by an enlarged comprehension of *relationships* of objects to himself. The stunted or deformed tree had its parallel in the wounded animal or man: asymmetry was hence a condition to be avoided, symmetry a quality to be regarded as normal. *Art has thus been integral with the pattern of life.*

Like life itself, art in its fundamental aspects is built upon human experience, which has surprisingly many common elements the world over. The common experiences lead to the development of similar cultures. Hence the art forms have tended to exhibit similarities and common character. Progressing from simple forms to more complex forms, the art of any period may, however, upon analysis or study, be found to be structurally simple *in essential design.* The particular directions which the development of art forms have taken have been diverse, but the fundamental qualities embodied in all good art[1] remain very much circumscribed. Man himself exhibits similarities. His behavior in its more elemental aspects arises from a limited number of psychological *motives.* Food, shelter, mating, congenial association with one's fellows, recognition of one's accomplishments—such, among others, are his universal primary interests. Success in attaining them yields satisfaction; failure or apprehension of failure to satisfy the

---

[1] These will be discussed subsequently. It is recognized also that strictly regarded there can be no 'bad' art.

need prevents peace of mind. Nature, moreover, presents the same prospect to all. The heavens, the occasional storm, the forests, wild beasts—all these affect man within limits of variation in much the same way. Some of the experiences arouse fear, others wonder; others leave him unmoved. Usually he responds in some manner, and, more frequently than not, the response involves adjustment of his behavior to the situations before him. To facilitate such adjustment he was wont to rely upon his past experience, adapting it to the present need and, if this was found inadequate, projecting it into the future. Hence arose the early crude stages of religious feeling in which his art played a part. Though still but imperfectly known, brief attention to it here may serve in our effort to comprehend some of the early functions of art.

2. The Known 'Beginnings' of Art[1]

The finding of fragments and even many intact expressions of the art of primitive man has been followed by a patient piecing together of significant phases of his art experience. Most of the discoveries date from A.D. 1879, when the small granddaughter of Señor Sautuola happened upon the paintings of bison (which she excitedly described as "bulls, bulls") on the ceiling of a cave near Altamira, Spain. Primitive art and its meaning soon became a matter of considerable interest. Evidence has been uncovered not only on both slopes of the Cantabrian Mountains, the Pyrenees, and other parts of Europe but in widely separated parts of the earth from eastern Siberia[2] to South Africa and the Americas (Fig. 1).

---

[1] For convenience, reference is made to 'beginnings' and 'origins'; the references, however, are merely to manifestations of early art that, through excavations and accidental discovery, happen now to be known.

[2] Spearing, H. G. *The Childhood of Art.* London: Benn, 1930, 2d ed. 2 vols.; Luquet, G. H. *The Art and Religion of Fossil Man.* Trans. by J. T. Russell, Jr, New Haven: Yale University Press, 1930; Burkitt, M. C. *South Africa's Past in Stone and Paint.* Cambridge: Harvard University Press, 1928.

The art of primitive man has extended to the drawing, painting, or graving of images of animals; the depiction of herds in motion and of the hunt; the decoration and adornment of weapons, tools, and utensils; the fashioning of small

FIG. 1. Bison and other animals drawn with black pigment on the side of a cave at Niaux (Ariège), France. *Photo by La Salle, Toulouse. After Spearing, courtesy of Ernest Benn, Ltd., London.*

objects; and the carving or modeling of figures and animals. Excavated refuse heaps have yielded utensils, bones of animals, shells of sea food, tools, and other accouterments of living. From that material, definite ideas of his existence may be surmised. The study of the culture of primitive peoples now living has provided us with the remaining knowledge needed to reconstruct the life of primitive man.

Upon the *character* of the gravings on weapons and rock surfaces most dependence must be placed for our interpretation of the mental life of prehistoric man. His life can be known only by inference[1] based both upon living primitive peoples and upon man as modern psychology has come to know him. Prehistoric man left no printed record, for language as we know it has existed for only the last two thousand years, printing just during the past five centuries. Human intelligence had to await that development before it could make the vast strides leading to our present civilization; since arts, literature, and science were not possible of development without the permanence of record and systematic transmission of ideas that a phonetic-symbol language system provided, making available for each new generation the cumulatively amassed stores of knowledge of the past. Of this primitive man knew little. His life was uncertain at best, and to the extent that peace of mind was found at all it was found in art and in religion.

3. THE CHARACTER OF EARLY ART

Our brief consideration of early art will be restricted largely to that which is best known—that of the peoples inhabiting the slopes of the Cantabrians and the Pyrenees during the Paleozoic geological period, twenty to thirty thousand years ago. Not being agriculturalists, they probably existed on animals, which were to them a constant source of danger as well as of food. Equipped with the poor weapons then known— the spear, the dart thrower, and the stone knife—the primitive hunter was no match for the ponderous hairy mammoth, the

---

[1] FROBENIUS, VON L. *Kultur-geschichte Afrikas*. Zurich: Phaidon-Verlag, 1933, is typical of comprehensive presentations of art as an important phase of primitive culture. See also GOLDENWEISER, A. A. *Early Civilization*. New York: Knopf, 1922, Chaps. IX and I, and SEABY, A. *Art in the Life of Mankind*. New York: Oxford, 1928, Vols. I and II (5 vols.).

charging bison, or even the angry reindeer. Against these he could not successfully cope without considerable peril to himself.

Paintings and gravings of these animals comprise the greater portion of his art. Only about one in five objects of his artistic interests extend to human figures—practically none to 'landscape,' 'still life,' or cultural objects. It is, therefore, of prime interest to observe that the normal objectives of his art interest were identical with the objects of his greatest fears. These must have been, inferring from normal psychological principles, continually in mind. The objects would be recurrently provocative of misgivings and, on the other hand, of constant concern as to manners and methods for coping with them. With that state of mind persisting through innumerable generations, there would come naturally some wish of a kind that would place dependence upon an unknown and invisible source of aid. The problem was thereupon projected, and to serve the desired end primitive man gradually conceived the naïve religio-mental frame of mind known widely as *sympathetic magic*. It is based fundamentally upon the observed close association of image with object, of shadow with that causing the shadow, of reflection with that reflected. Its objective is to gain control or in some way to be able to exert influence over the other. If he could but obtain some pictorial token of the object of his fear, his limited discernment told him— something that he could carry with him in control or view at length in security, having it as a constant reminder of his rise to ascendency over his quarry or feared object—he would feel better. In time this feeling amounted to a growing *confidence*, a mental advantage that may well have become a real advantage. Where odds are fairly even many a contest has gone to the side which, not bothered by futile waverings, believed with confidence it would win. Hence, by carving upon the walls of his cave where he habitually took refuge from the animals or sojourned during long, severe cold seasons, he was better able to visualize and contemplate the nature of the beast before him, to study at length, and in the end to benefit by a slowly rising feeling of confidence. The feeling came in time to be bolstered up gradually by something beyond confidence, a belief in a supernatural and inexorable influence which the image was believed to have over the animal itself, an identity of connection difficult for modern man to understand. Working in that pattern of emotionally motivated thinking, primitive man carved many fine designs on his dart throwers and on his hunting knives (Fig. 2).

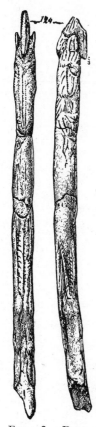

FIG. 2. Dart throwers in reindeer horn. Tarn-et-Garonne, France. *After Cartailhac, Courtesy of Yale University Press.*

Possibly some instances of the art of primitive man were animated simply by a desire for representation of his habitual environment, or at least of interesting portions of it. This belief is indeed held by several anthropologists, but if it were true, it leaves the question unanswered as to why four-fifths of these pictures are of animals and practically none of mountains, trees, caves, or utensils. Furthermore, it does not explain why there are so few portrayals of the animals in peaceful attitudes, since most of them appear in attitudes of wished-for prey (many later ones depict the hunt) or as stark realities connoting fearsome qualities.

The simpler interpretation is that he directed his emotionally driven concentration upon the vital elements of his existence. Such an interpretation, moreover, fits perfectly into known facts of living primitive peoples and furthermore tends to explain both the instances wherein remarkable expressiveness is obtained and the abstract character of symbolic figures well realized. The life of early man was too simple to be specialized in any way.

FIG. 3. Rock painting. A fight, apparently for possession of a bull. Thargur Tahl, Libyan Desert. *Courtesy of Museum of Modern Art.*

4. EXPRESSIVENESS IN EARLY ART

Observers of these pictures have marveled at the grace, movement, simplification, absence of superfluous details, gen-

eral expressiveness, and other features that suggest consummate skill. When we contrast the artist of that period with the
artist of modern times, there is, however, little occasion for
perplexity. The artist today has in his lifetime an infinite

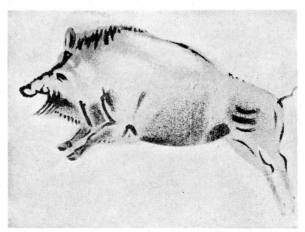

Fig. 4. Wild boar. A remarkable representation of rapid movement. Altamira
cavern, Magdalenian period. *After Spearing.*

number of stimulations that are meaningful to him. His possibilities for selection are greatly complicated. The very complexity of modern life makes him doubly susceptible to the
error of including too much in his picture. It becomes very
difficult to eliminate detail.[1] The situation with primitive man
was very different. His life was simple. Science, invention, and
technology had not come to clutter up his world. What he
saw he saw simply. Much of that which he did see made little
impression because he had not the finely organized cortex for
handling multitudinous associations that modern man requires and uses; but there was one class of objects to which he
necessarily became supersensitive: those things that meant to

---

[1] It was probably this very condition that contributed to the launching of one
form of Impressionism, which consists essentially of an insistence upon the
elimination of details and the placing of emphasis upon a simple, unitary
impression.

him food or danger. These objects he noted with a freshness and keenness of vision that enabled him later to create a graphic expression of his reaction on the wall of a cave or other surface. His furtive viewing of the hairy mammoth from con-

FIG. 5. Wolf. The technical aspect of this painting is curious. The whole background was first colored red and the wolf drawn on it in black and toned by careful scraping. It is not difficult for the present-day observer to imagine this as depicting a wolf cautiously emerging from cover. Cave of Font de Gaume, Magdalenian period. *After Spearing.*

cealment was an emotionally charged experience, leaving its memory image so well established as to make revival for the purpose of painting relatively easy and, what is more impor-tant, *accurately expressive* of the animal's pose at the moment (Figs. 4, 5). Hence, the painting we now find thousands of years later exhibits a rare quality in art which contemporary artists would be happy to secure. It is surprisingly akin to the successful efforts of artists of any period—results from that never-ending striving for dynamic qualities, for the 'spirit' of the thing. Because the painting was motivated by human emotions and experience, chiefly fear and hunger, common to all peoples, the picture is equally appealing to present-day man (Fig. 6). Fresh vital impressions, though of quite a different mold, are likewise frequently found in the drawing efforts of children.

Fig. 6. Rock painting. Khotsa cave, Basutoland, South Africa. The animal forms are elands. *Courtesy of Museum of Modern Art.*

5. Symbolic Abstraction in Primitive Art

The other striking characteristic found abundantly in the art of extinct primitive peoples is a symbolism that is expressive of abstracted qualities. On first acquaintance, one is impressed by the fantastic nature of the totemic figures.[1] However queer and incomprehensible they may appear to the uninitiated, they are in reality natural evolvements of the mental, emotional,

---

[1] Sloan, J., and O. LaFarge (ed.). *Introduction to American Indian Art.* New York: Exposition of Indian Tribal Arts, Inc., 1931, 2 vols.; Frobenius. *ibid.*; Guillaume, P., and T. Munro. *Primitive Negro Sculpture.* New York: Harcourt Brace, 1926. Good examples are observable in the American Museum of Natural History, the Field Museum, and the U. S. National Museum. Extensive bibliographies accompany the Sloan and LaFarge reference.

and religious life of prescientific peoples. They have not separated plausible illusion from reality. Their inner experiences, when reacting to the environment, have been subject to the same distortions and exaggerations to which the mind

FIG. 7. Totemic figures. These reflect tribal relations with indigenous birds, animals, and people. Haida Indians, Northwest Coast, North America. *Courtesy of Field Museum of Natural History.*

of anyone occasionally is subject. The material for art of this type is found in borderline experience, that which lies between clear and definite sensations and vague, confused ones that readily lend themselves to fantastic (to the uncomprehending observer) interpretation normally guided by traditional beliefs and supported by indigenous fears. A strange animal or bird or fish seen in semidarkness or mist or glimpsed in subwaking moments takes on a strange form, in one instance having exaggerated wings, in another having uncommonly large and bright eyes or perhaps peculiarly small and staring ones. Perhaps the distortion takes the form of a composite figure with a peculiarly shaped nose (Fig. 7). Once the experience becomes externalized in a carved and painted figure, it may take on, during successive generations, a slowly changing form,

FIG. 8. Model of totem pole (gíáah) erected near Kassett by Sqîlaǫ, a noted chief about seventy years old. Haida Indians, Queen Charlotte Island, British Columbia. *Courtesy of Field Museum of Natural History.*

merging into a legendary 'construct' totemized by having attitudes established toward it on the part of the tribe. The legend may grow, expanding in several directions, and may be perpetuated with regularly recurring ritual and ceremonials.[1] These art objects commonly serve a mystical function in making the individual more confident in his daily living and contribute toward a feeling of oneness with the group in which he lives. Even in their crude way they make for a better orientation in a world but dimly comprehended and imperfectly understood (Fig. 8).

6. ART AND EARLY RELIGIOUS EXPERIENCE

With the Druids the dolmen[2] served probably as altars. Conceivably, they may have been places where the troubled individual or clan could repair for a simple ritual through which

[1] For an account of the cannibal bird dance of the Kwakiutl, see Sloan and LaFarge (ed.). *op. cit.*, "Indian Masks," by C. C. Willoughby.

[2] Large, narrow slabs of native rock set on edge. In some instances a slab was placed on top of two or more resting on their edges, forming a crude shelter. These may still be viewed in some sections of France and the British Isles.

they secured renewed courage and with it some degree of peace of mind.

The intimate connection between the art of the group and concern for tomorrow is well illustrated in practices of the Pueblo Indians of the Southwest. For centuries they have held dance rituals characterized by slow, rhythmic movements, accompanied by a chanting chorus of old men huddled in a group, the rhythmic tempo set by the beating of a skin drum. Although referred to as a 'dance,' it is essentially a formula of deep religious supplication expressed with strong emotion. A zealous regard for exact performance of the ritual bestows upon it a primitive solemnity.

FIG. 9. Pueblo pottery. Zia, New Mexico. The rain-crop symbolism is expressive of the quick, brief showers of semiarid regions. From the author's collection.

The pottery of the Pueblo Indians also discloses the close and intimate connection between concern for tomorrow and their art as expressed in an objectifying of their prayers in the form of symbols. On their water jars and prayer-meal bowls, they place stylized dragonflies, frogs, deer, cloud forms, rain, and growing plants. It is not difficult to identify the primitive magic present in the symbols. The summer rainfall symbol is obviously a prayer for rain that may fall in time to benefit growing corn; since dragonflies are found about springs, pools, and water holes, their stylized forms on a water jar constitute a prayer that the jar may never be empty. The snake dance of the Walpi is the perpetuation of a religious ritual founded upon a legendary episode reminiscent of Germanic legends.

The Pueblo Indians still employ sympathetic magic in their dances and in their pottery, apparently unaffected by decades

FIG. 10. Potlatch bowl. This large bowl, modeled in the form of the seal as the symbol of abundance, is used in the periodic ceremonial feasts of the Chinooks. All guests are served from the bowl, with a large ladle which is also modeled characteristically in a form having special significance to the chief. Northwest Pacific Coast. *Courtesy of Field Museum of Natural History.*

of close contact with Anglo-Saxon civilization and the return of younger members from schools and colleges. Rain magic is invoked by a symbolic rainbow over a mountain, by the plumed serpent believed to dwell in storm clouds, his tongue being barbed lightning. At other times they live in lakes or walk to Indian dances on mist streaks. Figure 9 illustrates designs used by the Southwest Indians.[1]

The art of the African Negro and of Polynesia has recently received considerable attention, and many fine examples of their sculpture in wood have been taken out of Africa in recent times. Contemporary students of African Negro sculp-

---

[1] An enlightening study of the symbolism in Southwest Indian pottery is available in *The Pueblo Potter* by Ruth Bunzel, who spent two seasons with the Indians of Arizona. Reproductions of the symbols found on Southwest Indian pottery are included in the appendixes.

The two-volume monograph, *Introduction to American Indian Art*, published by The Exposition of Indian Tribal Arts, Inc., New York, is a comprehensive collaboration of data on the American Indian and should be studied by anyone who desires a trustworthy view of the subject.

ture[1] are inclined to discover in the distortions and indigenous stylistic peculiarities certain aesthetic values heretofore inadequately appreciated.

Doubtless in fashioning a figurine or head, the African worker in wood was motivated not by realistic reproduction of a model but rather by an emotional striving toward an attainment that may convey fully and effectively a deep religious feeling. Figures often suggest a primitive expression of the jungle atmosphere. Figurines, such as a specimen found in Gabun, serve the possessor as a fetish or small idol. Its significance cannot be fully understood except in relation to ritual, or magical potency through which its owner secures aid in his undertakings. Again the reader must bear in mind that the primitive artist is concerned with limited and simple reactions to nature.

Fig. 11. Balinese figurine. *Collection of Jan O. M. Broek, Berkeley, California.*

He is not disturbed by the multitudinous objects that tend to confuse a member of modern society or with involved conceptions of aesthetic dicta or with restrictive tenets regarding the construction of an object of art.

In other instances, the connection between religion and art is marked by an incidental utility that possibly is not recognized by the participants. On the island of Bali and in other

---

[1] Illustrations of these pieces with some interpretive comments are available in a publication of the Museum of Modern Art, New York: Norton, entitled *African Negro Art*, edited by James Johnson Sweeney; also in Frobenius, *ibid.;* and in Guillaume and Munro, *op. cit.*

parts of the East Indies, a periodic ceremony consists in designing and constructing elaborate funereal pieces. For important members a beautiful edifice is built to a height of eight or ten feet and mounted upon poles. In this the dead are placed, to be

Fig. 12. Balinese funereal pieces. *From photograph by Edward Bartow, Iowa City, Iowa.*

burned on the day of the ceremonies. This cremation act, in a land where cholera, bubonic plague, and other pestilences may have an outbreak at any time, serves a useful purpose, which, however, may not be consciously recognized by the participants.

It should be noted that the burial huts and cabinets of the Balinese are patterned somewhat after the native scenes, especially the indigenous flora. The materials here suggest the design, as also in other regions. The architectural edifices of religion have quite commonly taken on the character of the material available—hence the solidity of the Pyramids, the massiveness of the Babylonian, and the high and wide columns of the Egyptian edifices. The wide walls and stone facings have provided places for inscriptions and graphic history. The cliff dwellers constructed their sun altars of native stone, the Haida Indians their totem poles of the cedar or spruce tree. These devices are art enterprises that render man distinct aid toward continuing his thinking in a given direction and *provide some degree of continuity to life.*

7. GENESIS OF AESTHETIC FEELING

If we now turn back to earlier primitive art to a time when the first crude pottery was fashioned and the first carving of surplus weapons was undertaken, we may assume that as life became less and less nomadic and as primitive man became more and more freed from the hand-to-mouth existence characterizing earlier periods, reflection or contemplation of one's own work became more frequently possible. A well-balanced dart, a perfectly symmetrical arrowhead, or a crude pottery dish so well proportioned and shaped that nothing spilled from any portion of it came to be regarded *with more satisfaction* than those productions imperfectly made. In time, the artisans who consistently turned out better and better products would be the more admired and more frequently given the task of making weapons and utensils for others. The more man understood skillfully turned objects and weapons that were not only good to handle but good to look at and that in use sped more accurately and swiftly in flight, the more satisfaction primitive man got from those qualities.

The thesis, therefore, seems plausible that in the age-old admiration for work of consummate skill may be found the *basic pattern of aesthetic appreciation.* It is a matter of common observation that, for the clever stunt, the skillfully executed act, the much admired rhythmic running stride of the athlete, or the working of the master artist, applause is well-nigh universal. Though it is a far cry from the act of the tumbler to the studio labor of a Rubens or Titian, the same human expressions of admiration are elicited,[1] perhaps different more

---

[1] The observation of Elbert Hubbard: "Art is not a thing apart; art is just doing a thing well," expresses a similar viewpoint. (The relation between constitu-

in degree than in kind. The close relation of the subject matter of classic Greek art to *activities* of the period, particularly in the decorations of the Parthenon friezes, is a classic illustration.

The ability to do and the capacity to evaluate the product (aesthetic appreciation) are also probably closely related, as indicated by several lines of evidence. The good artist is also the able appreciator. If he furthermore possesses unusual language ability he may be a good critic or contest judge. Simply because he may be inarticulate in suitable words to describe his reactions is no indication that he does not have the critical ability to appreciate.[1]

If our attention is now directed to the findings of philology, it will be noted that the significantly earliest words according to Vendrye were not nouns but *verbs*.[2] Evidence exists that word symbols indicating to dig, to scratch, to anoint, and other activities preceded symbols for objects to be dug, scratched, or anointed. And when the name for sun appears in a later era, it is the 'measurer.' Activity thence pointed the way. Muscular exertions with attendant rhythms, which have aesthetic significance, quite properly had an early utility. In all probability the early stone shapers, the arrow-point makers, and the potter who fashioned the bowl by hand became aware of the effect of rhythmic action patterns and of simple regular repetition as contrasted with spasmodic effort. Even in present times, music has been used to pace cigarette workers; track athletes have learned the advantages of timing the stride.[3] Rug weavers

---

tional developmental susceptibility for art and heredity will be discussed in Chap. 4).

[1] It will be developed in a later section that the most important possession of the effective artist is aesthetic sensibility or the capacity to recognize aesthetic values. The artist, to be successful, must depend upon his own innate sense at every turn in the progress of his painting to guide him in its development.

[2] Trans. by P. Radin. *Language: A Linguistic Introduction to History.* New York: Knopf, 1925.

[3] Paavo Nurmi, one of the greatest runners of all time, is reported as having car-

of China maintain rhythmic work movements, particularly the tying of the knots, by the time and rhythm of an ancient chant. In such practice, rhythm came to be enjoyed for both its utilitarian advantage and its intrinsic satisfyingness. Hence, in the action phase of mankind's early experience, of which he was later to become vaguely conscious, there grew the rudimentary sense of a simple aesthetic quality—rhythm.

Even as the modern artist achieves satisfaction in successful attainment, so the artisan in all ages secured pleasure in contemplation of his successful handiwork. The satisfaction derived from contemplation, moreover, was not the only basis of aesthetic feeling. In his observations of nature and in the *repeated* contacts with significant aspects of nature, a lesson in appreciation accrued that was destined to be of tremendous importance in the genetic development of man.

As man's growing comprehension of nature expanded to more and more objects he was able to note repetitions that were the same year in and year out. It became something he could depend upon; something he could understand. Pattern —a conceived and comprehended Order—became a part of his gamut of experience. At times it was the pattern of waves rolling in; at other times the undulations of prairie grass when the wind blew or the pattern left in the sand by wave motion. These came to be recognized as normal conditions; experiencing them afforded him peace of mind. It was experience *in which he could place constant dependence.*

He also noticed that the human body in normal health is bisymmetric; that if a fellow creature had lost a hand, an arm, or a leg, he was no longer a person in possession of his full effectiveness. Such observations, extended to trees that in normal conditions are roughly bisymmetric, recognized that the tree whose branches had been shattered by lightning or

---

ried a clock for a considerable portion of the race, discarding it when it had served its purpose.

now had stunted branches from growing in an unfavorable location faced survival at a serious disadvantage. The tree having roots exposed by the erosion of a swift stream came to be recognized as a tree that was insecure and would soon topple into the stream. Those primi-

tive people living in mountainous regions came to learn that some mountains are fixed and relatively changeless; others having precipitous slopes would be likely to produce the avalanche or the thunderous snowslide. In that manner, a rudimentary comprehension of *symmetry* and *stability* came into existence. Seeing an object as unstable or asymmetric

Fig. 13. Carved wooden dish. Befum, Cameroon, Africa. *Courtesy of Field Museum of Natural History.*

would give rise to feelings of uneasiness and of insecurity. These feelings are even today considerably nonconscious, but they probably still are basically causative of the preference even in small children for the *symmetrical* and the *stable*.[1]

Constant experience over ages of time with symmetry and asymmetry, balance and unbalance, rhythm and arhythm, both in the activities of the individual and in his contemplation of objects round about him in which these qualities resided, afforded the basis in the physiological and mental structure of man for our present-day aesthetic feeling. These qualities therefore are only in part ontogenetically acquired; their basic character resides in something very primal, deep-set, and elemental.

A discernment of *consistencies* in nature was probably one of the first factors in changing an uncertain existence to one *marking the beginnings of an ordered world*. It provided something which was an advantage in both *greater attendant satisfaction*

---

[1] Evidence for such preferences by children will be discussed in Chap. 2.

in contemplation and *aid* in man's manipulation and invention, just as today the most efficient and fastest airplanes are also the sleekest and most beautiful planes.[1] So in the life of primitive man the best made utensils, the best made tools, and the best made weapons were those that provided also the greatest satisfaction in contemplation.

8. ART AS ORDER

An important function of art in the life of primitive man was then as now an objectifying or externalizing of experience in permanent form. Cognizance of the quality of permanence led to a perception of Order. The Order was observed as existing both in his handiwork and in nature. Recognition of it gave him a feeling of well-being. By nature he strove toward those conditions that would bring about such feeling and sought to avoid those that did not. Balance, perceivable in infinite variation; rhythm, appearing both in behavior manifestations and objectively, again in countless forms; and perhaps other simple aesthetic feelings uniformly and unvaryingly attracted him. Unbalance and arhythm regularly set up a state of unrest, or vague uneasiness, correctible usually by altering the situation or by removing himself from the scene. Through infinite repetition of such experiences with their consistent character becoming better and better known, based on the consistent models afforded by nature, man came in time[2] to have these fundamentally basic reactions.

---

[1] Abundant examples of the transition from early crude models to later highly efficient and beautiful forms are supplied in Sheldon Cheney and Martha Candler Cheney. *Art and the Machine*. New York: McGraw-Hill, 1936.

[2] Time is here conceived of not in centuries but in tens of thousands of years. The theoretical postulations are in harmony with the basic evolutionary doctrine of orthogenesis, which does not presume direct heredity but a *directional* tendency that makes it possible for succeeding generations to *acquire* the basic reactions more and more easily. A social factor, of course, operates also as the more immediate agent.

At a later stage in development the groping for Order merged into a sensing of *fitness*, again stimulated and nurtured by the models set by nature. The leaves surrounding the flower were observed to be of color and texture that appeared pleasing in juxtaposition. The colors of the landscape merged gradually into the more distant vista and then into the sky. Tinges of sky blue were intermingled as reflections in the grass, in tree leaves, and the surface of lakes. Some objects seem to 'go with' other objects or particular backgrounds more pleasingly than with others, and that easy blending of contiguous part with part which we now call *harmony* came gradually into man's conscious awareness. The total effect of 'belonging together' pervading the entire scene came to be known as possessing the quality of *unity*.[1]

On the other hand, the strewn wreckage following a severe storm or a landslide or the trampling of a savage herd were scenes viewed with misgivings. They were disturbing. By contrasting experiences, man found that when his things were 'in order' he could more readily find his needed weapon, better carry on his affairs. When the landscape was serene, he was serene.

In great probability the psychological explanation of man's preference for the unified, the fitting, and the harmonious rests upon the maxim of *least effort*.[2] Any scene that is disordered, confused, discordant, or rankly inharmonious produces in the observer feelings of vague discomfort. To correct the situation requires effort—frequently distasteful effort. On the other hand, the scene that is ordered, that is composed of related elements or elements that harmonize

---

[1] Modern Gestalt psychology postulates a comparable relationship, the unifying function of figure with ground. Experience is not acquired in discrete order, but as a pattern or relational existence.

[2] *Cf*. WHEELER, R. H. *The Science of Psychology*. New York: Crowell, 1940, pp. 38–40.

(fitness), produces in him a feeling of well-being. There is no need to put forth effort to correct the situation. He comprehends it easily. His inspection passes from one element to the next with little effort (sequence). There are no baffling dead ends, no jarring color notes, no puzzling arrangement or unjustifiable inclusion of superfluous objects. Everything in the situation suggests its natural relation to everything else. It must be understood that a situation *may* be so perfectly composed as to be 'uninteresting.' Perfect unity may be obtained by placing a cube in the central area of a rectangular area. This observation, however, does not vitiate the general premise, since such a scene would cause no annoyance, only pleasant feeling, though slight in degree. The value of the theory as outlined lies in its applicability to *any scene of any degree of complexity*. Interest and boredom are subjective states applying to individuals on particular occasions. This quality of 'holding together,' of fitting and appropriate elements in harmonious settings, whenever found in unit organizations capable of being easily and readily comprehended with definite feeling of pleasure, has in recent times been given the designation of *organic unity*.[1] Since it is so elemental a response, so much in accord with known psychological reactions, there is no good reason for assuming that it has not operated at least in an elementary manner with primitive man. Today, in a vastly complicated cultural setting, its function is greatly enhanced.[2] The need for unity has likewise greatly increased. With primitive man it tended to become a trustworthy guide to his own artistic practice, where it signifies the highest advance in his mental-emotional process in the contemplation of Order.

---

[1] The *names* of objects *exist in the social milieu*. There is no absolute relation between the time the word symbols have been in use and the time the experience it describes has been consciously known to man. Obviously considerable confusion is assignable to failure to realize this point.

[2] *Cf*. The Whitford Terminology Committee Report. Federated Council on Art Education, 1927.

9. AIDS TO THE CONTINUITY OF EXPERIENCE

As people—for protection from danger, communal agri-culture, or other motive—came more and more to live to-gether, and as the individual came to identify his personal welfare with the general interest of the group, art was utilized freely to give permanent character to regularly held practices. Religiously executed rituals and ceremonials contributed to a deepening feeling of solidarity—a feeling of group gain through faithful performance. The craftsman members[1] were more in demand to fabricate masks and costumes for the priest class, to decorate persons and construct habiliments needed in the ceremonials. A priest class, properly instructed, came to be an important factor making for an oriented outlook on life[2] and giving to every individual member a continuity and depth of thought not possible of attainment in earlier epochs.

Deeds of valor, successful encounters with dangerous animals such as the lion or elephant, and glorified heroics were per-petuated in pantomimic dances. The artisan was called upon to fabricate the needed properties; perhaps in many instances to perform the dance himself after the demise of the hero. In time the character of the performance underwent gradual change. The hero came to be a legendary figure—in some instances a godlike creature. He took on the character of a lion, a wolf, or a 'cannibal raven' of enormous size and power. The new aspirant to chieftainship was expected to make his pilgrimage to some remote mountain fastness alone, there to spend weeks in communion with the original godlike creature,

---

[1] These are believed to have been fairly numerous in some cultural periods of ancient life. *Cf.* HEWETT, E. L. *Ancient Life in the Southwest.* Indianapolis: Bobbs-Merrill, 1930.

[2] It must be borne in mind that much of the magical practices of primitive peoples, though appearing naïve from the point of view of twentieth century sophistication, is logical and defensible on the ground of providing for the group at that time and in that situation a workable scheme of social control, frequently resulting in conditions of serenity not found in some modern civilized settings.

in time to return possessed of the secrets of his power which he would on the proper ceremonial occasion demonstrate to the group.[1] The ceremonial unified the group, provided it with a periodic emotional outlet, and made it possible to have hereditary continuity in the perpetuation of its cardinal objectives.

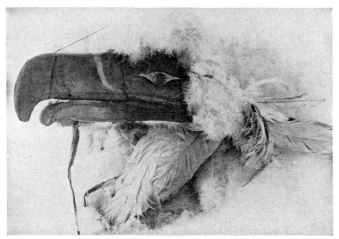

Fɪɢ. 14. Wooden mask, set with bird skins and feathers. Used in the "whirlwind dance" of the Kwakiutl Indians. Tribal authority of this Indian group resides in hands of the Hamatsa, or cannibal society. Accouterments such as these are employed to give continuity to the rites and impress the group. Pacific Northwest Coast. *Courtesy of Field Museum of Natural History.*

Following the New Stone Age and during earlier historic times, permanent records in the form of architectural structures, on which were engraved legends or group events of importance, appear in various places. Students of archaeology have been piecing together more and more of these artifacts of the earlier existence of man. Accumulations of such findings disclose the intimate relation of art and the life of man. In more recent periods discovery and study of additional evi-

---

[1] In the larger museums may be observed the headdress and other habiliments that have been used in ceremonials in contemporary primitive groups. The term 'primitive' herein refers to a stage of culture and not to any particular period of time.

dences of communal living in the past have proceeded rapidly in regions that have for the most part escaped attention. Recent structures and the accouterments of some states of culture ranking among those of the Near East have been un-

FIG. 15. Codfish ceremonial mask. Kwakiutl Indians, Pacific Northwest Coast. *Courtesy of Field Museum of Natural History.*

covered in Mexico, particularly in Yucatán.[1] Among the edifices at Chichen Itzá, Xochicalco, and other localities in Mexico and parts of Peru, the temples, stadia, and fortifications survive the culture of which they were a part. Here, as in other areas in different parts of the world, the religious ceremonials utilizing the sacrifice, the dance, music, and decoration made art prominent among the important activities of group life.

10. Art in Later Religious Experience

In the more advanced primitive group, life was less simple. Folkways grew into *mores*, through which the daily routine of the individual was strictly regulated. Customary ways, rather than individual judgment, governed conduct. In a society so

---

[1] See Joyce, T. A. *Maya and Mexican Art*. London: Studio, and New York: Boni, 1927.

thoroughly regimented, primitive religion easily attained a predominant position. Among some of the African peoples the use of masks, painted designs on the body, and 'properties' of bizarre design having magical significance exercised strong

Fig. 16. Whistles used to create sound of the unseen spirit. Tsimshian Indians, Pacific Northwest. In forest regions these are effective properties of the priest clan. *Courtesy of Field Museum of Natural History.*

control and served the priest class in their mediations with misfortune and adversity. The rhythm of the dance was augmented by the chant of the assembly or select group, and awesome sound effects were provided by concealed 'bull-roarers.' The designs usually were suggested originally by nature, particularly fearsome creatures. In their making and remaking they underwent a gradual mutation until they were stylized into symbolic form. In many instances the original source was lost sight of even to the oldest members. Psychologically, the symbols served as attention-fixing devices. Man is not able to carry complex and abstract ideas for long without the assistance of objective 'constructs.'

The altar and the temple, creations of the artisan planner, serve admirably as attention-fixing structures. With the Toltecs and Mayans the Sun Pyramids were places where sacrifices were made before the assembled group. Anyone in its presence was conscious of its special function. Sufficient evidence has been uncovered to indicate that the priest class in now extinct groups exercised remarkable ingenuity, working with the artisans, to impress the others with their supernatural prowess. Hewett in his excavations of Pueblo Bonito in Chaco Canyon (northwest New Mexico) has discovered secret passageways leading to an altar in full view of the amphitheater which made it possible for the priest to effect an apparently inexplicable appearance.[1]

In oriental life the temple has occupied a prominent and continuous function, with the prayer wheel, the sacred stone, or other objects on which the devotional interest came to be attached or toward which it was directed. The Japanese have placed temples in pine-tree and mountain settings, effecting in that manner a rare combination of religious sanctity and pure aesthetic satisfaction. The temples of Indo-China and of India express the basic religious attitudes of their builders.

The artist class of any age has thus been an active and important factor in creating the objective embodiments for widespread and diverse religious practices. In many instances the artist has been more than a close collaborator; he has been one of the participants in the rites. And it should not be overlooked that with the rise of symbolic practices, even in primitive societies, under the leadership of the witch doctor, the 'medicine man,' the shaman, or other functionary, a measure of ordered social control has been introduced in many instances resembling that in more modern states. Although the practices have been faulty in their logic and naïve in their theology, the

[1] HEWETT. *ibid.*

social gain considered in the light of the needs of the group has been real—indeed, quite significant.

11. ART AND THE CHURCH

The union of art and religion in the Western world perhaps witnessed its highest culmination during the Middle Ages. The great cathedrals of central and western Europe—like those of Milan, Cologne, Amiens, or Chartres—arose during this time, rather than at an earlier or later period, primarily because of the prevailing Christian attitude. The artisans, artists, and decorators regarded nothing of greater importance or significance to themselves than the opportunity to glorify the Deity by devoted labor in stained glass, carved or painted figures, or masonry. It was then a way to salvation. Magnificent façades, elaborately carved altar pieces, striking detail work about chancels, carved figures of the apostles—all these the work of many generations of continuous striving—stand as a lasting monument to the faith of those participants. Art then was a part of living. It was not merely a collection of objects to visit on Sunday afternoon, or attendance of a Friday evening recital. The Church was the vital center of community life, taken for granted and accepted without reserve. The great accumulations of movable pieces of art of the period also enriched the world's art: thousands of madonna paintings, articles used in the church service, and articles with religious significance for secular resting places. The symbols and attention-fixing devices went through innumerable mutations: usually arriving at some more beautiful design or more satisfying and frequently simpler motif. The design of the cross passed through many stages, tending now toward more ornateness, later toward greater simplicity, but constantly seeking still more beautiful design and aesthetically satisfying proportion.

Not by any means confined to western Europe, the stimulus of church interest in bringing art into all places has reached out to remote parts of the world—to the high Andes or the Philippines. Frequently it embodies the sole contact with art that

FIG. 17. Cathedral, Rheims. *Underwood-Stratton photograph.*

some isolated communities have. In modified form its influence dominates Indian architecture in the Southwest of the United States.

Music has followed a course parallel to that of the arts of design and architecture. Its service as an adjunct to religious practice is well-nigh universal, providing in no small measure emotional character and atmosphere. The religious experience would be robbed of its full significance without the emotion-inducing appeals that art and music together contribute. Even in primitive religion, ritual has often merged imperceptibly into art, and art has on other occasions formed the basis for a developing ritual. The chorales and chants of medieval church music are aesthetic experiences today whether in church or secular settings.

12. Integration of Experience by the Child: Child Art

The observation is now and then made that a striking resemblance exists between the art of primitive man and the art of the child. Owing to widespread interest manifested in the United States and Great Britain in the activities of Franz Cizek of Vienna, who has been guiding children through art activities for two decades, much discussion of the nature and potentialities of child art has been stimulated. In recent years, research has been directed toward a better understanding of the conditions under which children are creative. According to Cizek any child has the capacity to express his experiences creatively. If he does not, Cizek asserts, it is the pedagogy that is at fault.

Creations of children from all sections of the world where educational facilities have made possible their study disclose a wealth of child ideas that are vital, in some instances humorous, and in other instances clever.[1] In many of them definite aesthetic merit is demonstrated. The conditions under which these drawings and paintings were made are in most cases not known. It is probable that these productions represent the best from a large number produced by all kinds of children,

---

[1] The large world-wide collection exhibited in New York City in 1935 was analyzed by A. Anastasi and J. P. Foley, Jr. ("An Analysis of Spontaneous Drawings by Children in Different Cultures." *J. Appl. Psychol.*, 1936, 20, 689–726.)

being, therefore, exceptional rather than typical products and, in some instances, not completely uninfluenced by adult mediation.

Extensive studies made in normal public school situations in the United States have shown that, when children have been given the liberty of choosing what they wish to paint, although the subject matter is restricted somewhat to themes arising from fairy tales and stories that all children know at a given age, supplemented by things seen in the community, they produce a great variety of pictures. Perhaps only one out of twenty of these would be classified as creative in the sense that it represents something unique, vital, and unusual.[1] Most children even at the ages of six to nine tend to express themselves in a more or less stereotyped manner. Some children express themselves in creative ways at any age, but they comprise a small minority. There seems to be, therefore, little scientific substantiation of the Cizek thesis that *any* child, if left to himself, will produce an abundance of creative products. Even Cizek's children must profit from suggestions unavoidably obtained from seeing the work of children displayed on the walls and from the criticisms of Cizek himself. It is, however, altogether probable that any child will respond to judicious training and under favorable conditions will produce many interesting drawings or even paintings. It is also to be observed that children's failure to produce creatively may be attributable to some extent to the lack of suitable materials. A sharply pointed pencil is not a suitable tool for the child, whereas clay for modeling or soft chalk or tempera paint may, in the hands of many children, stimulate activities of a superior type.

With the very young child, a distinct phenomenon occurs which is almost wholly unrelated to artistic production in the

---

[1] Investigations made by the author and assistants. Studies in the Psychology of Art, Vol. I, *Psychol. Monogr.*, 1933, 45, 63–81.

usual sense. The child at the age of two or three normally engages in random activity with the crayon or pencil which, to the adult, is apparently meaningless. Such products usually go by the name of scribble. As the child matures, however,

Fɪɢ. 18. Child's tempera painting. Boy, age six. This was produced by a talented child. Graphic-concept development of this degree would ordinarily be reached by children several years later; by many, not at all. See also illustrations of children's work in Chap. 4.

some of this scribble takes on recognizable form, and, even where it does not, the child when interrogated may assign a title to it even though the title may seem fantastic to the adult.

As the child matures still further, into the fifth or sixth year, and particularly if a rapid maturation of motor skill accompanies the mental development, the products will more and more resemble recognizable objects. A rectangle with two spools under it will become a train or car, an elongated oval with a circle at the top will become a man, to which in time will be added two lines for legs and two other lines for arms. Some children of course develop these forms much in advance of others and are very industrious in their production of them.

At the ages of six and seven some children will produce even elaborate drawings of figures or objects such as trains, auto-

mobiles, airplanes, or boats. When large areas are available to
work upon, such as a blackboard or large sheet of paper, the
child may draw a house with children playing in front of it or
almost any kind of compositional assembly. A feature of these
products is that the child in the front yard will often appear to
be larger than the house, or that the furniture in the house will
be plainly visible through the walls. These are not errors in
perspective, nor should they outrage the adult's sense of
proportion. The child is not engaged in naturalistic representation; he is simply using graphic means for *consolidating and
integrating his developmental experiences.* With each drawing of a
boat or plane he is learning more about those objects. His failure to complete his drawing satisfactorily at one instance
stimulates him to notice details about the locomotive the next
time he sees it; hence it follows that next time his drawing will
be better. Through that process he extends and enlarges his
visual concepts of his world. He draws those things in which he
is interested, and he draws them in the proportions that interest him. Hence, other children are far more important to him
than a house or tree, and he is interested more in getting the
children into the picture. Furthermore, he *knows what is in the
house.* Therefore, he draws it in, oblivious to the fact that it
bothers the adult to see objects in the pictures that do not
appear from a definite vantage point.

In time these supposed errors correct themselves. The child
slowly perceives the spatial relationships as does the adult. It
is usually, therefore, pedagogically unwise to attempt an exposition of the laws of perspective to a six-year-old child, who
simply is not interested and furthermore has not the capacity
as yet to grasp its significance.

The art of the child is therefore like that of primitive man
in some respects and quite different in others. At its best, it
has the vitality and expressive accuracy frequently found in the
art of early man. On the other hand, it lacks the workmanlike

character and finish of the primitive product. It is also not
related so emotionally and directly with the vital necessities of
life as must have been the case with primitive man. In the use
of materials the work of early man discloses resourcefulness
and the employment of graving tools seldom utilized by the
child. The former in many instances was motivated by a
philosophic or religious interest that could hardly enter to any
real degree into the child's reckoning. With primitive man,
therefore, the art activities were deadly serious; with the child
they enter largely into the play aspect of life and serve inci-
dentally to consolidate and integrate his developing or growth
experience.

13. SOCIAL CONTROL THROUGH ART

Man is prone to permit his behavior to be guided by what
others are doing or by others' behavior that may afford a suggestion for his.[1] Insofar as behavior is not logically arrived at—
and that includes probably most of one's behavior—the suggestions coming from pictorial material are many and frequent. Caricature may undermine a good reputation in the
casual thinking of the multitude. In the same way an unim-
portant man may be elevated to a position of importance by
the judicious and continued play of caricature that presents
him in a favorable light through repeated suggestion. Perhaps
no one has the potentialities for effective suggestion more than
does the satirist working through the medium of art. The weaknesses and shams of contemporary life have been a matter of
permanent record through the pen and brush of Daumier,
Hogarth, and the less artistic but effective Thomas Nast. In
contemporary affairs, many have felt the sting of critical scorn
by the pen and brush of George Grosz and of contemporary
newspaper cartoonists such as Kirby, McCutcheon, Ding

---

[1] The notion is the central theme of the French school of social psychology in
which Tarde is the dominant figure. *Cf.* his *Laws of Imitation*.

(Jay N. Darling), Fitzpatrick, and Duffy or the functional distortions of Covarrubias.

The satirical artist must therefore be a person of superior social discernment who not only comprehends current affairs but with a mastery of understanding is able to see the inconsistencies or vagaries in the situation and formulate them in graphic terms that utilize the common perceptions of the masses to express and parade forth these aberrations of individuals or society. They are vastly more effective because they present their criticism in picture form, which is intelligible to nearly everyone. The cartoon, moreover, offers the possibility of combining rich humor with criticism and is thus true satire. The cartoons of Jay N. Darling are often inimitably humorous as well as devastatingly critical; in fact, so much so that even the object of the deadly barb can nevertheless enjoy the humor himself. Such exceptionally effective cartoons represent social control at its best, because the control is administered in a manner that leaves no resentment.[1]

In less serious aspects of life, art plays a leading role in suggesting the preferred types of feminine beauty or masculine prowess. The classic figure of the Greek athlete is still an object of admiration and emulation. In minor ways and for shorter periods the prevailing type of beauty was established by various major and minor artists. The type appearing in Titian canvases represented the preferred type of his time. The Rubens type featuring the full-bosomed, sensuous, and matronly figure is distinctly in contrast with the tall, narrow-waisted 'Gibson girl.' The frail, thin, willowy girl made popular during the decade following the First World War through the drawings of John Held, Jr., and Marge represents a still different influence.

---

[1] A recent study of the cartoon and editorial as propaganda carriers, however, disclosed that the cartoon that is too entertaining is less effective as propaganda than one crudely drawn but embodying a deadly attack. ANNIS, A., and N. C. MEIER. "Effectiveness of the Cartoon and Editorial as Propaganda Media." Unpublished Manuscript.

During the advent and sway of the latter type it was common to find excessive dieting and other restraints upon normal growth in vogue. The extent to which the feminine population follows the leadership of a few artists and dance exponents is well known. The process involves the cooperation of fashion magazines and others regarded as 'smart' and of general interest to women. These reflect the preferences of stage and movie stars and women of fashion whose suggestions are widely followed.

The tendency to adorn oneself in order to present oneself to one's fellows and win admiring attention is not a phenomenon peculiar to modern times. It may be observed in the lives of any people, even savages in almost any part of the world. It has taken various forms, including restrictions of one's person —such as the binding of feet, the burdening of ears or nose with ornaments, reshaping the head, or the application of paint and other decorations to various parts of the body. The original motive rests with the individual, but the burden of thinking up newer and more original designs and schemes for ornamentation falls especially upon the artistic element within the group. In contemporary life the function of the make-up artist in the beauty parlor in every community of importance has become one of increasing importance. In the production of motion pictures and stage plays he is perhaps the person of paramount importance. One sees not the natural beauty of the individual but rather a construction of the make-up artist prepared with a view toward the necessities of appearance on the screen or before the footlights.

Although beautification processes may not typify great art, it should be borne in mind that art is not to be identified with easel painting and sculpture alone. The arts of design include vastly more. Even the arrangement of a dinner table involves careful planning and evokes aesthetic judgment. The dictates of good taste are not wholly an individual enterprise; they

must be subservient to the same universal principles that
operate to determine value in a good painting.

14. ART IN INDUSTRY

Zealous proponents of 'modernism' recurrently tend to see
'awakenings' of an interest in 'new' design and loudly herald
the advent of the new theme or tendency, naively assuming
that a revolution in design is at hand. Within the last two
decades metal, glass, and leather were the new materials that
were to replace 'obsolete' materials. The materials governed
the design. To be alive to real art one was expected to embrace
the new themes without reservation and with complete disdain
for that of the past.[1]

Good design, however, is not a matter of progressive change.
It is stabilized in no period. The 'latest' in motorcar design
may or may not be the most beautiful. And a costly twentieth
century gown or piece of furniture may be aesthetically
inferior to one of the time of Columbus.[2] The handmade guild
products of the Middle Ages are still widely imitated, as are also
ancient Chinese and Persian rug designs. Products of common
need that have had the attention of countless designers and
craftsmen prove to be good or not good through the presence
in the thing itself of a number of qualities. Material that is
suitable to the purpose, good balance, unity of design, other
basic elements functioning appropriately—these factors usually account for general acceptance as good art and give to it
the aesthetic quality that makes it satisfying to the beholder as
well as to its creator.

---

[1] In perfect fairness to the more intelligent and balanced leaders, however, it must
be said that current enthusiasm is in most instances motivated by a sincere desire
to find *new and better* design.

[2] See *Psychol. Monogr.*, 1933, 45, 147–184, for evidence on this point, wherein it
was found that even untrained subjects preferred some seventeenth century
gowns to 1920 and other more recent models (Jacobson).

One may inquire why it is that only after considerable experiment does society arrive at a satisfying design, as witnessed by the airplane of 1915, and present types; or the bathing costume of the nineties, as contrasted with those of today. The answer must be that these are in a sense special cases: the one had to await the development of suitable materials (for instance, duralumin) and the other a change in social standards and to some extent new materials (rayon, rubber fabrics, etc.). Furthermore, the human mind works slowly when it is confronted with new problems. The tendency is usually to think in terms of the present, and when the shift is toward a new use of a principle there is always the likelihood that the new lead is a mistaken one. Efforts to build an airplane by imitating the bird met with failure when the attention was fixed upon the *wing* as a source of *propulsion*. The use of a lightweight engine as the source of power was applied only to the wing idea as a *glide sustainer*. The creators of airplanes finally accepted the engine as a *pulling* motive force and adopted the body of the fish as the correct fuselage idea, since both must slip through a fluid (water, air) with a minimum of resistance from the fluid that surrounds it. The present-day Boeing, Douglas, Lockheed, Martin, and Messerschmitt planes are highly efficient machines; *they also are strikingly beautiful*. Compared with their predecessors they are in design greatly simplified, well proportioned, and perfectly balanced.

The automobile is an example of the relation of beauty to utility. The first automobiles were merely horseless carriages: an engine was placed under the seat and a chain and sprocket (suggestion from the bicycle) carried the power to the rear wheels. The dash with its whip socket remained for a time; only the shafts were omitted. Tops were later added, fashioned after the surrey top. When a means was devised for getting the power carried that far the engine was relocated in front of the driver—after all, it replaced the horse, didn't it? For two decades the automobile was a creature of gradual evolution away from the carriage idea, but its design as a true automobile is only of recent origin. The suggestions for change were in most cases tied up with developments of adequate propulsion. About 1925 with the advent of the Chrysler car radical changes became frequent and a low-hung, sleek body design became the order of the day. With efficient and powerful engines realized, body design came to be of first importance. It was not alone the impetus toward lessening wind resistance that impelled new body designing; it was the recognition of a general demand made in no uncertain terms for a *better appearing* car. The rivalry of the three largest producers of popular cars for public acceptance on a basis of appearance became one of the high points of the industry.

In no other field are designers more alert, more eager for new ideas, and more driven to produce them. Although the design has shifted more since 1925, the improvement has not been a straight-line development. Mistakes have been made, wrong assumptions adhered to, and unwise tendencies persisted in, until the invariable check—sales decline—turned them away in search of better design. One prominent make in 1929 built a model with bulging sides and rounded corners to get away from severe lines and sharp angles. But the changes were not made in relation to the whole design; and, although the car was mechanically satisfactory and business conditions even more prosperous than the preceding year, sales fell off to the extent of forty per cent. The experience taught that the car must be regarded as a unit: one part cannot be altered without serious risk of affecting the whole.

New ideas of car design are not plentiful. Time and again the new crop of models announced annually discloses similarities that suggest a tendency to copy the design of the previous year that had the best sales record. If the lines of the radiator run horizontally six out of seven makes will have them. Even the broad general principles of car design are not yet well understood. Should it be like a teardrop, a bird, a fish, a greyhound, or a bullet? It is interesting to note that, although the airplane has successfully been designed as a fish with exaggerated side fins, the problem of the automobile is not identical. It is not even similar. The automobile is a conveyance for one to six persons who want to sit upright in a comfortable position and be able to see forward. To follow the fish motif, so successful in the airplane, the automobile would need to be not fourteen feet long but forty to permit any approximation of the airplane proportion. Traffic conditions do not permit this. Furthermore, there is no functional necessity for a tapering rear which in the airplane carries the rudder and elevators. Although the so-called 'airflow' design was an attempt to break away from conventional design it was not successful. Since conditions do not permit any automobile to be driven safely on highways at speeds one-fourth as fast as transport planes, the functional necessity for excessive streamlining is perhaps more fancied than real. Quite significant is the fact that one of the oldest and most successful (also beautiful) cars has never attempted radical streamlining and maintains its traditional design in essential character from year to year. Any adequate explanation of the consistent success of this design must include the observation that it rapidly attained a satisfying basic design early and has been constantly checked and rechecked along the line of sensible application of aesthetic principles that, when applied, take into account the effect upon the total unitary impression. Any radical attempt to rebuild the automobile on the pattern of the racing greyhound or the running rabbit is inviting serious difficulty simply because the analogy may not be apt.

Design, let one remember, may work two ways. In order to redesign a car to lessen wind resistance the designers may find to their chagrin that the product suggests in mass the tortoise!

And if they model their creation on the basis of a leaping greyhound, they may find they have erected some disturbing blockers of cross winds! Some of the experimental designs look well in clay or wood but create difficulties for the mechanical engineers. Other models have been frankly accepted as transition models, not satisfactory to either the artists or the engineering staff. The bulletlike body may be feasible only if the passengers are willing to lie down or sit on the floor; otherwise, the teardrop or slipstream motif must remain as a suggestion to the eye or partly realized as a *tendency* in design.

Without doubt, advances in metallurgical science providing the designers with materials capable of standing strains and stresses not found in present materials will revolutionize design still further. It does not follow, however, that mere redesign or any radically 'new' design will be better or more beautiful than designs heretofore known. It may be—if the design motif is at the same time identical with aesthetic considerations.

15. Art in Political Control

In a way that is strongly reminiscent of the cave man's effort to carry with him an image of a feared animal or hated foe and thereby gain some measure of control over it, modern nations have likewise attempted to objectify their gains over former enemies. Hence, they attempt systematically to perpetuate the symbols of conquest and thus foster a feeling of ascendance over their rivals. For this purpose, they have used sculpture and the memorial in varied form. In most European cities one may find equestrian monuments to illustrious generals commemorating victory, or memorial arches under which triumphant soldiers still march on every suitable occasion. These permanent monuments tend to stand as constant reminders of the prowess of the people and to centralize the nation's thinking on national holidays. They are furthermore utilized occasionally to cement alliances. The erection of monuments to fallen heroes of the other group is followed by pilgrimages and periodic deputations to renew the feeling of solidarity. As in religious shrines, the graves of war heroes may be made hallowed places where delegations and distinguished individuals may visit with attendant ceremony.

Contemporary spectacles in which art has been utilized in colossal proportions have been used with great effectiveness in Nazi demonstrations in Germany. The massing of participants, the design of the rostrum, and the massing of martial sound and lighting effects creates in its total effect a spectacle of mighty power.

In lesser character, governments have used art in propaganda for the purpose of discounting opposed social organizations and glorifying their own social system. The Russian communistic system has been shown as a vigorous and righteous youth, whereas capitalism was portrayed as a decrepit and iniquitous person. In countries where illiteracy is high, symbols that can be easily shown on banners or billboards have been widely seized upon to carry and fix slogans in the minds of the people. Many ideas otherwise not easily conveyed to an illiterate population may thus be made available by pictorial means.

As a controlled agent of government, art may degenerate to crude or simple propaganda, or it may rise to the heights of dramatized social consciousness. Art, however, is art, dependent upon whether or not it conforms to certain structural requirements and has certain expressive characteristics. It can have this whether the subject matter be national aspiration or any of the ordinary trivia that have occupied the interests of artists in the past.

BIBLIOGRAPHY

Balch, E. S. *Art and Man*. Philadelphia: Allen, Lane & Scott, 1918.

Bulley, M. H. *Ancient and Medieval Art: A Short History*. New York: Macmillan, 1926, 2d rev. ed.

BURKITT, M. C. *Our Forerunners*. New York and London: Holt, 1924.

BURKITT, M. C. *South Africa's Past in Stone and Paint*. Cambridge: Harvard University Press, 1928.

CASTLE, W. E. *Genetics and Eugenics*. Cambridge: Harvard University Press, 1916.

CHENEY, SHELDON, and MARTHA CANDLER CHENEY. *Art and the Machine*. New York: McGraw-Hill, 1936.

DE ROCHEMONT, RUTH. *Evolution of Art*. New York: Macmillan, 1929.

ELLIOTT, HUGER. *Fashions in Art*. New York: Appleton, 1937.

FAURE, E. *History of Art*. Vol. I: *Ancient Art*. Trans. by W. Pach. New York: Garden City Publishing Company (Harper), 1937.

FRAZER, J. G. *The Golden Bough: A Study in Magic and Religion*. New York: Macmillan, 1907–1915.

FROBENIUS, VON L. *Kultur-geschichte Afrikas*. Zurich: Phaidon-Verlag, 1933.

FROBENIUS, VON L., and D. C. COX. *Prehistoric Rock Pictures in Europe and Africa*. New York: Museum of Modern Art, 1937.

GARDNER, H. *Art through the Ages*. New York: Harcourt, 1926.

GARDNER, H. *Understanding the Arts*. New York: Harcourt, 1932.

GOLDENWEISER, A. A. *History, Psychology, and Culture*. New York: Knopf, 1933.

GOLDENWEISER, A. A. *Early Civilization*. New York: Knopf, 1922.

GOLDSCHEIDER, L. *Art without Epoch*. Oxford: Oxford University Press, 1937.

HADDON, A. C. *Evolution in Art: as Illustrated by the Life-histories of Designs*. London: Walter Scott, 1895.

HARRISON, J. *Ancient Art and Ritual*. London: Williams & Norgate, 1913.

HEWETT, E. L. *Ancient Life in the Southwest*. Indianapolis: Bobbs-Merrill, 1930.

HIRN, Y. *The Origins of Art, a Psychological and Sociological Inquiry*. New York: Macmillan, 1900.

JOYCE, T. A. *Maya and Mexican Art*. London: Studio, and New York: Boni, 1927.

KNIGHT, R. P. *The Symbolical Language of Ancient Art and Mythology*. New York: J. W. Bouton, 1892.

KROEBER, A. L., and T. T. WATERMAN. *Source Book in Anthropology.* Berkeley: University of California Press, 1920. Chaps. 4, 7, 10, 26, 28, 29, 30, 42, 43, 50.

LALO, C. *L'Art et la vie social.* Paris: G. Doin, 1921.

LUQUET, G. H. *The Art and Religion of Fossil Man.* Trans. by J. T. Russell, Jr. New Haven: Yale University Press, 1930.

MARCH, C. "Evolution and Psychology in Art." *Mind,* 1896, N. S. 5, 441–463.

MEIER, N. C. (ed.). "Studies in the Psychology of Art," Vol. I. Chaps. by P. C. Daniels, C. Jasper, K. Whorley, W. E. Walton, and W. Jacobson. *Psychol. Monogr.,* 1933, 45, No. 200.

MEIER, N. C. "The Appreciational Arts—Art." Chap. XIII. *Yearb. Amer. Educ. Res. Ass.,* N.E.A., 1939.

MEIER, N. C. "The Graphic and Allied Arts." Section VIII of Child Development and the Curriculum. 38*th Year.,* *Nat. Soc. Study Educ.,* 1939.

MORRIS, E. G. 100,000 *Years of Art.* Boston: Stratford, 1930.

MÜLLER, K. O. *Ancient Art and Its Remains.* Trans. by F. G. Walker. London: Fullerton, 1850.

O'REILLY, E. B. *How France Built Her Cathedrals.* New York: Harper, 1921.

PELIKAN, A. G. *The Art of the Child.* Milwaukee: Bruce, 1931.

ROOS, F. J., JR. *An Illustrated Handbook of Art History.* New York: Macmillan, 1937.

SLOAN, J., and O. LaFARGE (ed.). *Introduction to American Indian Art.* New York: Exposition of Indian Tribal Arts, Inc., 1931, 2 vols.

SPEARING, H. G. *The Childhood of Art.* London: Benn, 1930, 2d ed., Vol. I.

THOMAS, W. I. *Source Book for Social Origins.* Boston: Gorham, 1909. Part I, Part V (Art, Ornament, and Decoration), and Part VI (Magic, Religion, Myth).

TOMLINSON, R. R. (C. G. Holme, ed.). *Picture Making by Children.* New York and London: Studio, 1934.

VENDRYE, P. *Language: A Linguistic Introduction to History.* Trans. by Paul Radin. New York: Knopf, 1925.

VIOLA, W. *Child Art and Franz Cizek.* New York: Reynal & Hitchcock; and Vienna: Austrian Junior Red Cross, 1936.

Chapter 2 · PRINCIPLES UNDERLYING ART

1. THE QUESTION OF PRINCIPLES

In Chap. 1 we have seen that art emerged with man even in remote parts of the world and that it has served universal needs and functions. Its universality and ubiquity have not been adequately understood, however. Our proneness to identify early art chiefly with the Egyptians and the Greeks is explained by the fact that the art of Egypt, of Babylonia, of Chaldea, and of Greece is simply better known to us than the art of other lands and of remote periods.

We have noted also a close relationship between simplicity and good art. The Greek temple, for instance, is a masterpiece of simple structure in which both the materials and the design were perfectly fitted to the purpose of serving as a dwelling for a god or goddess. Some of the cave man's drawings are aesthetically effective mainly by virtue of their simplicity. No doubt the clarity and absence of complexity explain in part the feeling of satisfaction with which we of the twentieth century view a reproduction of an Aurignacian bison painted by a creature to us completely unknown. Though we know little of the extinct races who once held forth in southern Mexico, for instance, we may greatly admire their designs on carved columns. Throughout the tremendous range and variety of art produced during the past thousand years in Europe it is

50

possible to appreciate qualities in the painting or sculpture without knowing the individual or the conditions under which it was produced.

Even though the appraisal of a work of art is ordinarily a difficult undertaking, it may still be said with considerable assurance that in the better art of the world there is discernible the *operation of a few simple principles*. They are *ingrained in human experience*, but *learning* enlarges comprehension of their more subtle and complicated functioning. In their simpler aspects, they are within the ken of children.

Strangely enough, however, there is more confused thinking concerning principles than on any other subject relating to art. Unfortunately, one finds diverse viewpoints. Some disdain principles; some believe they stultify art; some believe the greatest creative work follows when principles are left behind; some deny their existence. Some complain that art should always be left 'free' and never subjected to discipline or made to 'conform' to principles. Much of this confusion lies in a mistaken or a restricted notion of the nature of principles.

Principles, in the first place, should not be confused with *rules*, which are edicts given to the beginner with the expectation that they will help him avoid certain pitfalls and errors that usually have been found to occur. There are certain ways of dividing the picture space, certain rules to be observed in mechanically balancing dark and light. Closely related are the familiar rules of perspective that serve as a device for reconstructing nature in an artificial manner. In all art schools and in public art education, other more or less tangible and rigid rules have been advanced to aid the beginner. Some of these are simple admonitions, such as the presumed advisibility of not placing the head in a portrait too close to the frame.

In the second place, principles should not be confused with standards or canons of taste that concern the prevailing preferences of persons regarded as having authority in art precincts. Many superficial phases of art in advertising design, costume design, and illustration follow current trends. The prevailing trend is supposed to be in accordance with good art standards and good taste, and, moreover, to be clever, chic, or 'modern,' and associated with 'exclusive' shops on Fifth Avenue or the Avenue de l'Opéra. As a matter of fact, these trends have too frequently proved to be but transient preferences, that hold sway for a period only to be superseded by other trends. The newest steel-and-leather furniture may be in accordance with the recommendations of the highest paid design consultants—it may or may not be good art. Such canons of taste may refer only to particular groups and their followers and to particular periods of time.

Thirdly, art, like other cultural enterprises, is in varying degrees subject to the influence of traditions that may vary from period to period or place to place. The popularity of a particular medium may dictate the kind of art produced. At one time an egg tempera may lead to concentration upon only such subject matter and treatment as may work satisfactorily with the medium. Work done in other mediums less suited to the times or subject matter inevitably tends to suffer in comparison from judgments made by contemporaries, yet be differently appraised by posterity. In other areas fresco may be particularly in order; hence, evaluations should bear in mind that the medium determines largely the kind of subject matter and the treatment. The murals and fresco works of Rivera, Orozco, and others in Mexico need be considered, for full appreciation, in the light of socially inherited traditions (fresco medium from Italy and Spain), the socio-political ideologies, the architecture of the region, the climate, and the material in which it is placed. Anglo-Saxons have experienced a wide variety of reactions to these works: the reactions may simply express unconscious bias in any one or all of the above directions, preventing the observer's full appreciation of the art itself.

2. The Significance of Principles in Art

Contrasted with transitory trends and the limited significance of rules, axioms, traditions, canons of taste, and maxims in art, *principles* of art *are general qualities that inhere in all good art.* Quite contrary to the general notion that to take principles into account leads to a thwarting of initiative, it will be observed that principles need never indicate ways of organizing a picture in any rigid fashion. Principles are *qualities* that are *attained* by the artist. The same subject matter, as for example a mountain landscape, may be treated by a hundred different artists, yet each, completing his painting in his own individual manner, may have made use of the principle of rhythm, for instance, and *each will be found to have used rhythm in a different manner.* Hence the significant point regarding principles is that there are countless ways of attaining aesthetic results in which principles inhere, and these ways are limited only by the ingenuity of the painter himself. The highest art, therefore, will probably be that in which the *greatest number of principles have been most intelligently and aesthetically utilized,* within an effective unity. It is seen that principles in and of themselves may be barren of aesthetic value since perfect balance, for example, can be had by placing two trees equidistant within a rectangle. That would, however, be an unintelligent use of principles, and the result would be of little interest. The student seeking understanding of value in art will do himself great service by searching for the diverse and multitudinous ways in which artists of all periods and in all lands have obtained satisfying results. Insofar as these results rest upon formal elements, permanently satisfying organization, and not merely upon associations with objects or matters of local interest, it is most

probable that aesthetic principles more than any other consideration explain their value.

If it be granted that there is universal admiration for the
clever, the ingenious, and the skillful, then the greatest admira-

FIG. 19. Primitive design. Toruba carvings. West Africa. *Courtesy of Field*
Museum of Natural History.

tion goes to that artist who has *utilized principles in effective and
skillful ways,* not in stereotyped or obvious ways. Therefore,
the immature art student who slavishly attempts to balance the
psychological weights of elements in a composition or who gets
a studied and therefore artificial rhythm in placing color spots
or light and dark will not succeed usually in getting an aesthetically successful composition. Best results seem to come
when the student has given long study to the ways in which
principles *have functioned* in good pictures and has made this
knowledge a matter of second nature. When he has made this
a subconscious process, his whole attention may be given to the
manipulation of content to the end that the ensuing composition will disclose subtle and effective uses of rhythm, balance,
and other aesthetic qualities. This is tantamount to saying

that, when the attention of the artist is given to *aesthetically effective organization*, good balance, rhythmic placements, and other components of *unified* structure will more or less inevitably appear as a consequence.

It is therefore to be understood that balance may appear in a Japanese wood block, in a Persian rug design, in an Egyptian architectural structure, or in an intricately organized Cézanne still life or landscape. The balance may reside in the placement of colors or values; it may be found to exist in the placement or accentuation of line; but, regardless, it is still *balance*, in the same way that a Cézanne landscape or a Renoir café scene may have *rhythm* in fifty or even a hundred different ways.

3. THE PROBLEM OF TERMINOLOGY

There is no doubt that the art world would greatly benefit if agreement could be reached upon a satisfactory conception and listing of principles.[1] There would be less confusion also, if such a list were small, or if it could be shown that a number of principles could be subsumed under general principles of wide application; regarding symmetry and stability, for example, as special aspects of balance. However, even though a list might be agreed upon, it would next be necessary to educate the public into an adequate understanding of their nature and significance, for it is of greater importance to the student of art to learn how principles may function adequately and effectively than it is to learn a few definitions, since definitions tend to suggest rigid interpretations, particularly among the less intelligent. It is very significant, furthermore, to regard principles as being basically integrated with human experience —with experience that is normal, that man throughout time

---

[1] A praiseworthy enterprise in the direction was the report of the Committee on Terminology's study. See Federated Art Council's report (W. C. Whitford, University of Chicago, chairman of committee).

has been accustomed to find about him as normally conducive to a feeling of satisfaction; recognizing, moreover, that the symmetrical mountain peak, the butte, the evergreen tree, the snowflake, the leaf pattern, and countless other objects give

Fig. 20.   Fig. 21.

Fig. 20. Primitive design exhibiting aesthetic qualities of symmetry, radiation, opposition. Talish Indians, Vancouver Island, British Columbia. *Courtesy of Field Museum of National History.*

Fig. 21. Primitive design having repetition, sequence, opposition, and rhythm. Although this design is pleasing as viewed, it will appear to have a face in the upper half when rotated a half turn to right. Spindle whorls. Talish Indians. *Courtesy of Field Museum of National History.*

satisfaction to mankind today as in primitive times. The graphic rhythms in cloud forms, in waving grain or grass, or in the rolling surf and the auditory rhythms of the drumbeat and cadence in primitive dances—or in the music of the modern orchestra—have likewise served to excite a response that is to man normal. The rhythmic experience is ever a constant assurance of order and fitness.

Art need not be at all complicated. One needs only to observe that the statue evolved from the hewn tree trunk, examples of which may still be seen in the totem pole, and that the Greek temple had its origin in the simple hut of the Greek. Investigation reveals that complicated art forms evolved from simpler forms and that, in some of the most complicated and apparently involved paintings, one will find with brief study that they are laid out on the basis of a relatively simple pattern.

A number of contemporary artists and sculptors have gone back to the creations of children and of primitive peoples for suggestions, believing that art has become unnecessarily complicated and that it is necessary to get back to fundamental design and simplified form.[1] By so doing, these artists believe that they have attained a far more effective and forceful art since the appreciator can get more directly and fully into the spirit of the form.[2]

4. GENETIC EVIDENCE FOR THE FUNDAMENTAL CHARACTER OF PRINCIPLES

The extent to which principles are ingrained in human experience is disclosed in the reactions of small children. A series of investigations made on preschool children and in some instances continued into the grades and high school demonstrated that young children were responsive to situations involving compositional balance and rhythm. These studies were made with materials familiar to children and were put in the form of problems for the child to work on, his reactions disclosing whether or not he comprehended such things as balance or rhythm and also whether he preferred a balanced situation to an unbalanced one.[3] The rhythm studies included a large number of reactions to prepared materials. The results of these investigations clearly demonstrated that a child of five years, and in many cases much younger, responded positively to balance and indicated a definite preference for

---

[1] Barlach, Matisse, Schmidt-Rottluff—among others.

[2] *Cf.* GARDNER, H. *Art through the Ages.* New York: Harcourt, 1926. Chap. 1; VAN LOON, H. *The Arts.* New York: Simon & Schuster, 1937; FAURE, E. *History of Art.* Trans. by W. Pach. New York: Garden City Publishing Company (Harper), 1937. Vol. V, *The Spirit of the Forms.*

[3] Studies in the Psychology of Art, Vol. I (*Psychol. Monogr.*, 1933, 45, No. 200). See investigations by Daniels and Jasper. These studies base their findings upon behavior reactions rather than upon language. The chapters by Whorley and Walton will also be of interest.

balanced compositions. Similarly in the studies of rhythm, children at the age of five or six almost invariably preferred the rhythmic type of material.

Another study using clay models of landscape gardening material had for its objective the responsiveness of the child to problems involving compositional unity. In this instance most children did not show a very definite ability up to the age of eight years, although individual children between the ages of six and ten did exhibit a definite comprehension of the function of unity and in some instances developed their problems in ways comparable to solutions concurred in by trained adults. Color harmony was discovered as being more or less beyond the ken of children under the age of twelve; in individual cases, though, striking mastery of color harmony was evidenced. In these illustrations and in the products of children everywhere, it is evident that the production of good art, when allowance is made for immaturity in technical skill, is possible at almost any age. In the case of young children, the absence of the complicated trappings of civilization may partly explain the attainment.

5. The Problem of Art Criticism

The task of the art juryman in selecting a prize-winning picture from a large group of exhibited pictures frequently involves real difficulties. The outcome of the judgment has often led to acrimonious debate and in many instances to sharp disagreement on the part of the friends of the painter. So long as art value is regarded as a subjective matter entirely, there will always be lack of agreement. In some instances it has been charged that the decisions of the jury were definitely colored by personal relationships to the artist and even, in certain cases where some prominent artist has been on the jury, that he has used his persuasive powers in the interests of an art friend of equal standing, expecting that when the situation is

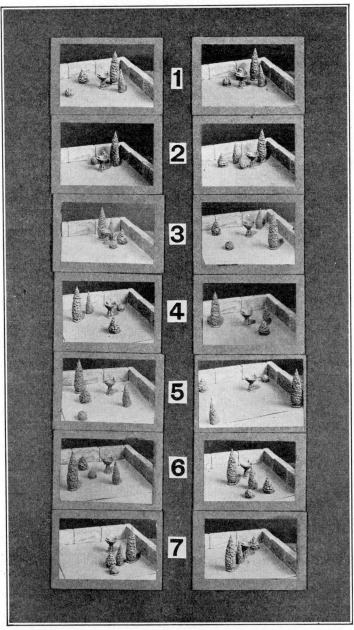

FIG. 22. All these arrangements (landscape design problem) were made by children at ages of five and six years, illustrating range. Those in groups 1, 2, or 3 are not materially different from the arrangement that would have been made by adult landscape architects. *After Whorley.* See page 58.

reversed his picture will receive favor from his friend. Of course such procedure is more or less subconscious and fortunately is not general. It is human nature for a juryman to look with favor upon a picture that has been painted after his own manner or to see in such a painting many superior qualities not equally appreciated in the others.

If art can, on the other hand, possess some degree of *objectivity* it will have that objectivity largely through a consistent understanding and ability to sense effective uses of principles in a composition. If judgments are made on that basis, it becomes possible for jurymen to see the same picture independently, yet along objective lines. In fact, it would be quite impossible for any art to persist from age to age *unless there were some qualities basically constant* in art judgment. The fact that good critics today can appreciate the work of Phidias or Dürer or Hokusai tends to suggest that there are objective qualities in the work of these men that do not rest upon any subjective likings for subject matter, materials, manner of work, or expressive significance. An experimental study on the consistency of aesthetic judgment tends to show that in cases where the compositions are themselves sound, the judgments made a year later tend to be consistent with those made previously.[1] Among artists generally, one finds definite faith in the reliance upon principles as providing definite criteria in art. Out of forty-one competent artists approached by the writer on the question of what constituted in their minds the most dependable criteria in art, all except three were inclined one way or another toward some phase of principles. Several of those having international reputations were extremely positive on the subject. It would seem, therefore, that any constant and defensible art criticism must rest upon a clear and thorough understanding of principles in art.

---

[1] Cahalan, E. "The Consistency of Aesthetic Judgment." *Psychol. Monogr.*, 1936, 51, No. 5, 75–87.

6. THE ELEMENTS OF ART

A work of art is built upon one or more of the three commonly accepted elements—line, form, and color, to which may be added tone (often referred to as value, light and dark, or notan). Texture is sometimes considered a basic element. Again, as in the case of principles, it must be understood that line, form, and color do not intrinsically make *art* structure. Their *intelligent use* leads to artistic creation. Line may be used merely as a scaffolding, or it may possess properties inherently its own, being used in some pictures to lend emphasis to the character of the object or to establish effective relationships within the organization. Line may also carry empathic states, since a fine, thin line may carry the suggestion of delicateness, a heavy line that of strength or harshness, and a jagged line of strong movement. It has been pointed out that there are no lines in painting, but for convenience the artist uses lines to mark off edges of areas. Artists vary greatly in the extent to which they utilize line either for structural purposes or for empathic purposes. The dynamic symmetrists make abundant use of line in the complete organization of the area—having diagonals from corner to corner and perpendiculars to other corners with many other interrelated line relationships. Modifications of the theory of dynamic symmetry include the use of so-called dynamic line as a means for securing a better unity within the frame and of keeping suggestive movement within bounds. Most of these schemes assume a two-dimensional surface or work on a basis other than that of regarding the scene as being a three-dimensional organization.

In academic forms of art where the rules of perspective are employed, the entire construction is based upon line. In this usage, line is called upon to serve the functions of reconstructing nature commonly as seen from a single vantage point. Certainly in compositions made up in part of architectural edifices, street scenes, and similar subject matter, line is almost a necessary aid in construction. It should be noted, however, that with the advent of the skyscraper and the airplane some artists have seen fit to introduce new types of perspective that are not readily comprehended by those trained in the low-horizon point of view. In the painting of still life, radically new developments have occurred in which the plane of the picture appears tilted. This is obviously a simple expedient of placing the eye level at a much higher point than has normally been done. Its obvious effectiveness is seen in the fact that it senses more of the three dimensions of objects than is possible from the eye-level point of view.

In recent years, art has also experimented with the suggestion of *line travel*, using the psychological effect of lines that point or that carry thrusts in a definite direction. The suggestion of very definite space relations is therefore obtained by having these lines of interest carry beyond and between elements in the picture so that the observer is trained to a perspective view that is taken from a relatively high point. To secure the same effect, the objects may be arranged in a staircase or structural order on a tilted curvilinear base so that many objects and interests not normally feasible in a straightforward, naturalistic composition may be brought into the picture plane.

Form refers to the aspect of a composition that carries the connotation of substance. If the composition is normally lighted, the forms will be those masses that cut off light and cast shadows. The surface arrangement of these areas of light and dark is usually referred to as the *pattern*. Form in a composition may be definite or vague. It may be heavily delineated or thinly outlined or merely suggested. The aesthetic character of the composition is somewhat determined by the balance of light and dark and the patternal distribution.

In some quarters there has been a tendency to regard form in a number of special senses. One use, which however is limited, considers form as a mass of interrelations between all objects in a composition. Obviously such use of the term 'form' in the sense of *unified whole* can but lead to confusion, since the term 'unity' is well established as a workable concept in art.

Still other uses of the term carry the meaning of structure and of style. As in poetry we have the sonnet or idyl, in music the tone poem or symphony; so, it is reasoned, graphic art should have its forms, the exact nature of which are not clearly indicated. 'Structure' is used also to apply to the organizational framework; likewise the term 'structured' as applying to the manner used by the artist in building the basic design. 'Architechtonic' is still another term applied to the structural aspect of subject matter, particularly in such examples as are constructed in deep space and involve three-dimensional character.

The third common element in art is *color*. To many, color is the primary element in art. Its function can be that of recalling the true appearance of forms within the picture; it can be used also to convey emotional character, to emphasize by contrast, or to convey the idea of distance through the functioning of the advancing character of some colors and the retreating nature of others. For instance, blue tends to suggest distance; red, warmth or something close at hand; grayed colors generally carry the eye beyond the immediate ground; fully saturated colors tend to suggest forms nearer at hand. Where dependence is not placed upon relative color or saturation of hues, the suggestion of spatial relations may be accomplished by manipulations of line and form.

In some quarters there is the inclination to include as elements light and dark or tone, and texture. At best, these could be merely special uses of line, form, and color. In the case of sculpture, however, and in certain kinds of oil painting, texture conveys information that is not readily ascribable to the three common elements.

7. ORGANIZATION

The use of line, form, and color in an artistic manner results in a totality that commonly goes by the name of *composition*. The success of the artist is directly measured by his relative effectiveness in obtaining an aesthetically satisfying organization. Arrangement and design are frequently used as synonymous with composition. Since the problem of the artist is to create an illusion of three-dimensional space on a two-dimensional surface, we may delay final consideration of the matter of good design until after we have reviewed some of the ways in which the artist manipulates visual space.

8. THE MANIPULATION OF VISUAL SPACE

It must be remembered that photography is a comparatively recent invention and that many of the fine works of art were done before photography became highly developed. Consequently, many of the early medieval paintings indulged in photographic detail. They also graphically reproduced stories representing historic events. Art today should justify itself in providing something that artistic photography cannot provide. We can note that at all times traditional art has been an effort to paint objects and persons that express some feeling of the painter toward the object. He has, therefore, needed to take cognizance of the way in which the human organism perceives the space about him in order that he, the painter, may duplicate somewhat those conditions on canvas. Consequently, he has noted in painting an outdoor scene that distant objects appear less distinct than near objects; that in certain times of year a distant scene appears as hazy or blue or purple in color; that an object cutting off part of another object, both at a considerable distance away, is closer; that the relative size of the object is an indication of its relative distance away; and that two parallel lines appear to come to a point in the distance. The psychologist who has been experimenting with spatial perception for decades had long known all this.[1] The artist, in mastering his technique, learns the way geometricians reconstruct nature from a high-level viewpoint or from usual positions and hence utilizes this constructed schema for his special needs. Perspective serves as an approximation of reality to most persons even though some people, traveling by airplane or viewing cities from skyscrapers above the ground level or usual point of view, have seen fit to criticize its usefulness. It has also been possible to suggest space relations on canvas merely by the selection of color hues and relative degree of saturation.[2]

9. THE CRITERIA OF AESTHETIC VALUE

We have now become aware that the work of art is constructed of elements producing in the end an organization that normally follows certain aspects of design. Stated in another way, it may be said that a satisfying work of art is one that conforms to the principles of good design. If we now relate this to the simple beginnings of aesthetic feeling in the days of early man, we may find that good design rests upon the attainment of a relatively few simple qualities. These may be simply rhythm, sequence, and balance with the many subforms such as those in the following outline:

---

[1] See texts on space perception in bibliography: Carr, Katz, and Luckiesh.
[2] The basic principle of synchromism.

RHYTHM	SEQUENCE	BALANCE
Repetition	Transition	Repose
Alternation	Graded movement	Equilibrium
Interrelation of lines, forms, tones, and colors without necessity of exact repetition	Progression	Informal (free, occult)
	Sequence of forms, direction, areas	Balance of line, form, tone, and color
Sequential flow	Color and tonal sequences	
Unison of movement		

Effectively used, the ensuing composition will possess the supreme quality of unity and if further examined will show that supreme attribute of *fitness*. Unity is the sum of all of the effectively attained qualities and goes by various terms suggested by different persons; as, for example, significant form (Clive Bell), expressive form (Sheldon Cheney), plastic form or plastic unity (Dewey, Barnes, and others), and organic unity.

Naturally it cannot be expected that unity alone will explain the appeal of a picture. As in the case of principles, a picture may be perfectly unified and still be uninteresting, hence the qualifying adjective accompanying the different kinds of unity as presented by different writers. Bell, no doubt, had in mind significant form as a resultant of the organization of some graphic theme in a significant or effective manner, not in an obvious or common way. Cheney and others believe that expressive form should convey some emotional state of the painter or sculptor—it should express or interpret some deep feeling of the person presenting it.

It is observable that there may be varying degrees of unity. It is obvious, furthermore, that since unity is a resultant of the *effective functioning of many principles* it is possible that many more principles could be operating in one picture than in another and that when a large number are functioning, the degree of approximation of complete unity is therefore increased—likewise its aesthetic quality.

No listing of principles can be inclusive or sufficient to account for every aesthetic attainment. Domination climax, inclusion finality, and cohesion relation have been advanced as major principles. It is possible, however, to regard these as special means of securing unity and as particular aspects of rhythm, repetition, or balance. *Emphasis*, likewise, may be regarded as one means of effecting unity and is of the same order as dominance. *Contrast* suggests balance in opposition.

That there is more likelihood of agreement upon criteria of value in art when the list of principles is small was one of the findings in a carefully planned study made at the University of Illinois by Llewellyn Wiley. Having subjects react to a variety of abstract designs (line) on a basis of pleasantness and "ease of seeing organization," it was found that artists could rate the designs reliably upon the aesthetic criteria of balance, rhythm, symmetry, and unity, even though the artists all used their own individual definitions of the terms. Correlations ranged from .69 to .90. Pleasantness ratings, Dr. Wiley found, are highly correlated with the ease with which one can perceive organization of the elements of the pattern. An interesting observation is that, in making a factor analysis of the variables, "correlations . . . suggest that 'ease of seeing organization' and rhythm are the same thing, so far as these particular designs are concerned."

In the works of the old masters and great painters of all times a study of the manner in which the success of the painting is attained will disclose the multiform manner in which balance, sequence, and other principles have been used. In Picasso's *Absinthe Drinker* (Fig. 23) a large number of instances of sequence appear in the form of transition from color to related color, of value to value, of movement. One can also

observe examples of interrelations of form such as appear in
the hair mass and folds of the cape; also rhythm of line,
rhythm of form, and repetition of color notes. Although the
picture is replete with instances of the effective play of

FIG. 23. Picasso, *Absinthe Drinker. Courtesy of the International Art Publishing
Company.*

principles, the total effect is one of a high degree of plastic
completeness. In another sense, the picture exhibits no note
that does not appear in place and no texture that does not
appear in harmony with the dominant figure. The plastic
unity, therefore, of the painting is a close interrelation of all
parts. In the instance of El Greco's *Madonna* (Fig. 24) one is
impressed particularly by the rhythms abundantly presented

in values, color, and line. El Greco has attained a delicate balance of suggested movement and elements in repose. One may find sequence in any part of the picture. The same color tone and texture is repeated throughout. Again in this compo-

Fig. 24. El Greco, *Madonna. Courtesy of the International Art Publishing Company.*

sition one finds a large number of the examples of the use of principles woven together to form an aesthetically moving unity. There are no disturbing areas and no textures unrelated to those dominating the picture, in fact, only positive values secured through the effective use of rhythm, sequence, and balance. In a wholly different way, El Greco had attained earlier the same effective unity that Picasso achieves today.

The appeal of the El Greco *Madonna* is not limited by the attainment of obvious aesthetic qualities. The lines of interest suggested by the tilt of the torso and counterthrust of the neck and head offer an interesting and effective balance of thrust and counterthrust. No doubt also the particular expression of the Madonna has considerable appeal to the typical spectator and the use of lighting on folds of the garment, shawl, and facial surface contributes toward the total merit of the composition. These considerations may be regarded as supporting devices in the complete attainment of a total unity and aid materially in the realization of the stability and perhaps other incidental qualities.

The thesis presented herein needs a word of caution at this juncture. Aesthetic experience has two mutually interacting sides: the object itself, and the reacting individual. It may even be considered as having three aspects: the aesthetic experience of the creator of the object of aesthetic regard, the object as it exists for an indefinite time thereafter, and the succession of individuals who thereafter may contemplate it. Of these the only permanent, knowable reality is the object itself.

As Orozco puts it, the art in an object does not change: *we change*. It may be added that not only do we change, but we all view the object in a different light to begin with, that initial experience being subject to individual backgrounds that can never be identical with two persons, living in the same or in different social milieus. The particular congeries of experience may lead one individual to view El Greco's *Madonna* with a strong favoring religious bias; another may be unaffected by that motive but like it because he has acquired a liking for the unique El Greco style and hence admires everything 'El Grecoish.' Similarly the individual familiar with French or Spanish liqueurs or wine shops or the type of roué or habitué depicted will undoubtedly find *enhanced* interest in the *Absinthe*

Drinker. The individual who has never set foot in Europe may find the character wholly unfamiliar, likewise the setting; yet his *aesthetic* experience may be equally rich and complete, at least comparably so, particularly if his appreciation of form is further developed. Both, moreover, could hardly fail to admire the object as a product of *skillful handling*, not alone technically well painted but as having achieved a measure of unity in the successful relating and integrating of all aspects— line, form, and color—into a complete art form. The common ground on which all individuals stand in their admiration of the work is hence basically the universal regard for skillful handling of means (in the dichotomy of things well done), but realized in the particular aspect of masterful attainment of a unity (dichotomy of Order) by successful and effective use of principles of organization.

Aesthetic experience, viewed in this light, places the emphasis upon artful attainment and that universal criterion of artful attainment—unity through organizing factors. Aesthetic experience hence is more or less independent of *knowledge about* the creator of the object. Such knowledge may serve to enhance the complete experience. It does not depend upon knowledge of the *setting* or *conditions* in which the work was created. It does not require knowledge of the relation of the work to social, religious, or political considerations that may or may not have motivated the creator. Again, such knowledge may enrich the aesthetic experience, but it is not vital to the experience itself.

The thesis has been advanced that proper appreciation depends upon the ability of the spectator to place himself *en rapport* with the creator of the work. A somewhat similar view holds that only those who have an appreciation of the problems of painting can ever fully understand the aesthetic experience. It would seem utterly impossible for many individuals to meet these requirements. It would seem utterly unreasonable to expect them to project themselves into the state of mind or feeling of Hokusai in *designing* his *Wave* or of any of the early Chinese artisans in designing their vases or ink paintings which now, as then, the world acclaims as great works. Painstaking research may permit the scholar to relive much of the probable experience of these men, but the significant fact remains that it has not been necessary to undergo that process to appreciate the art objects. They live as permanent acquisitions of mankind. They are responded to universally because of psychological similarities in man's own reacting structure independent of knowledge about their creators, who are in many cases unknown and about whom no inquiry need be made. The universal admiration for skillful achievement and realization of unity (order) is in itself sufficient. Although we change, our aesthetic attitude, if based on such premises, changes but little if at all. Our admiration of things well done is not vitally different from the admiration of generations in the past.

It still remains to be observed, nevertheless, that whereas the key to the explanation of merit possessed by a work will usually be found in the effective functioning of principles, it cannot be gainsaid that knowledge about the subject matter or analysis of the constituent structure of the work serves to enhance rather than degrade the individual's response to the work. Those in the audience who themselves sing or have extensive knowledge of the score are perhaps those whose enjoyment of opera is keenest. Mrs. Clair found that, after high-school art students had been led systematically through an analysis leading to a deepened understanding of paintings reproduced in full color, the experience almost invariably resulted in an *enhanced* appreciation.

A painting exhibiting deep dramatic qualities may have these same dramatic qualities as much from the organization as from the content. But the effect of the latter will depend somewhat upon the prior experience of the observer. Any person will be impressed with the high drama of Curry's *The Return of Private Davis*, by virtue of its somber realism, powerfully expressed (Fig. 25). The A. E. F. veteran who

FIG. 25. John Steuart Curry, *The Return of Private Davis. Courtesy of the artist and the Cudworth Post, American Legion, Milwaukee.*

experienced the effect of front-line carnage and heard the stories current throughout the times will see in the painting not only the return of a war 'buddy,' but the high-domed sky and procession of cloud forms on the distant horizon will arouse dormant memories of dismal rain and muddy fields and clearing sky. The legend of the Angels of Mons, concocted most probably from a distorted and overworked sensorium and fleeting, wispy clouds in the distance, together with boyhood imagery of angels, is now given plausible restoration to him. It all comes back to him now. His response experience will necessarily be different from the youth standing beside him, whose only contact has been through the pseudo reality of the Hollywood production. Yet all will be impressed with the somber drama and the subject matter, the experience in all being further deepened by the aesthetic qualities inhering in the arrangement. Hardly anyone could fail to appreciate fully the suggestion carried by the repetition of cloud forms on the horizon of marching men. No one could fail to be

Fig. 26. Cézanne, *Blue Vase. Courtesy of Braun & Cie, Paris—New York.*

impressed by the unity of the whole scene and by the fitness of all values to carry through the theme of the artist.

Principles thus present in any work of art—painting, literature, the play—tend to *reinforce* the dramatic quality. Powerful rhythms, dynamic contrasts (balance), with dominance and subordination (unity) tend to make the scene or the episode effective. If the design or the arrangement is at the same time simple in character, the probabilities are that the effect will be greater, since the operation of the principles will be sensed more readily and completely.

Although unity is theoretically a state of completeness in organization, it is probably seldom actually obtained. Perfect unity is, nevertheless, an abstract goal toward which great artists of all times have striven and, perhaps in some few instances, have to all intents and purposes attained. The experimental artist is constantly aware of ways in which he may improve his organization. Cézanne, for one, was constantly dissatisfied with his work, reputedly throwing his canvas in the ditch now and then on his way home; yet Cézanne, a thoroughgoing experimentalist in art, was one of the great artists who used color for structural purposes and worked long and assiduously to get arrangements into a degree of structural unity approximating perfection. In his *Blue Vase* one may imagine the effect of removing objects in the picture one at a time, conceiving what the picture would appear to be without that object. For instance, if the tall bottle on the left were removed from the picture, a serious dislocation of the picture would result. If the small red apple next to the vase were removed, the charm of the vase-and-plate relationship would be seriously disturbed. If the ivory-colored structural detail in the background were altered, considerable dislocation of relationships would ensue. In short, the composition is so neatly welded together that the disturbance of any one part can be done only at the expense of risking serious dislocation of the total unity.

10. EXPRESSIVE QUALITIES

Line is seldom perceived merely as line but as having qualities or characteristics that are read into it from having been associated consistently and regularly with situations and objects that have these same qualities. The characteristic quality is hence revived vaguely in the consciousness of the individual on seeing the line. The process is one aspect of the general process of conditioning. It occurs so casually in the life experience of the individual, however, that few if any are ever aware of its occurrence. Yet it is experimentally demonstrable that even children do sense some of the more common qualities in line, with adults exhibiting a wider range of responsiveness.[1] A thin line connotes delicacy, a heavy one strength. According to Lundholm the affective character of line has its origin in the suggestion of movement of the line, and this depends upon the idea that this movement in some way imitates the motor expression of an emotion. He states:

> Lines symbolizing states of strong emotion have short waves and acute angles, and lines symbolizing states of weak motor expression have long and low waves; and second, lines with waves of the former type and acute angles themselves suggest intense emotion, while lines with waves of the latter type suggest weak and slow emotion.

Concerning direction of emotion Lundholm further proposes that

> The downward tendency of a line expresses relaxation, the upward expresses power. The downward tendency expresses faintness, not sufficient strength to keep up. Going downward expresses losing of energy. The doleful line droops without energy. If it had enough force it would have ascended higher. Strength is expressed by going upward. A joyous line also ascends. Joy is an uplifting feeling. A forceful line tends upward. Thereby it attains the idea of ambition. A line indicating strength is a line tending upward, never downward.

The experiments of Poffenberger and Barrows indicate that from a considerable group of possibilities certain feeling states were more definitely recognized as representing close affective

---

[1] Walton, W. E. "Empathic Responses in Children." *Psychol. Monogr.*, 1936, 48, No. 1. Typical studies on adults are reported by Lundholm, Poffenberger and Barrows, Guilford, and others. See bibliography at end of this chapter.

relations to curves and angles than were others. The outstanding feeling states and the line character closely associated are as follows:

Sad—big curves tending downward.
Quiet—big curves on a horizontal plane.
Merry—medium curves tending upward.

Others show a somewhat divided association, possibly arising from experience of a varied character. Typical of these are

Lazy—big downward curves, or big horizontal curves.
Agitation—small, upward angles or medium, upward angles.
Dead—big, downward angles or big downward curves.
Serious—big, horizontal angles or medium, horizontal angles.
Powerful—medium, horizontal angles. or medium, upward angles.

From the foregoing it is indicated that the experience of mankind has not been uniform nor has there been unanimity in the consequent feeling responses. There is sufficient common experience with the more definite feeling states, as sad, quiet, or furious, to afford suggestions to the artist. It is no accident then that in expressing old age or deep humility or despair the lines of the figures would tend downward and would require large, easy curves. So designed, the response of the spectator would hardly fail to sense the expressed quality because it would be in conformity with his own prior observations.

Line quality will carry with it a suggestion of the quality that it has acquired in the normal experience of mankind, and the certainty with which it carries the quality is to a great extent dependent upon the universality of the experience and the depth of the feeling or emotion experienced. Likewise, certain forms that suggest or express qualities and colors may also convey moods or give some special character.

In this special associative aspect, known as *empathy*, the observer really feels an identity with the quality or character that the line suggests. These experiences are, by amplification, refinements and extensions of the original experiences of primitive man and are more or less inevitable in a complex world. The thin line suggests delicacy because lacework, embroidery, the spiderweb, and other objects depicted as frail are or appear to be made up of many fine lines. Similarly, the artist making a sketch of an outdoor setting in which he wishes to have fine lines and tracery to suggest the atmosphere of delicacy will probably find the weeping willow or some similar object in nature as his model. A rugged mountain form or a stone edifice would best be sketched in heavy, straight lines, whereas if movement were desired, the artist would use upcurving or spiral lines suggested by moving cloud forms and smoke spirals. Short lines that change considerably in direction carry out the idea of rapid movement. Vertical lines suggest dignity —horizontal lines repose.

Considering color, we find that blue, having been associated in mankind's experience with the sky and ocean, has come to stand for calm, restful qualities. Red, on the other hand, having been associated with transient and restless situations such as fire, is provocative of action and movement or restlessness and instability. Green, like blue, being a color found abundantly in nature, suggests restful scenes and quietude, whereas yellow on the other hand is like red, exciting and stimulating.

In the same manner, rough and rugged masses suggest qualities associated with brutality or force; smooth masses with qualities associated with ease, repose, or tranquility. A mass bounded by heavy black lines is often utilized by the artist to suggest powerful or rough character.

Variations of these essential qualities have their own character associations which in some instances are in accord with the widespread experience of mankind and in other instances represent only a limited experience. It would appear that the work of art having its 'expressive line' most in accord with the common experience of mankind or the work that utilizes the greatest number of these devices that carry emotional feeling would rank high. Not only would this general observation apply to the 'fine arts' but also to industrial design and the cartoon.

11. ABSTRACT VERSUS ASSOCIATIVE CHARACTER OF ART: GENERAL AND CIRCUMSTANTIAL

Somewhat apart from considerations of aesthetic qualities and expressive-associative character, the question is sometimes raised as to whether good art—enduring art—can be great if not conceived as abstract. The point of view would exclude from the realm of real art any naturalistic rendering depending for its enjoyment upon a knowledge of the setting on which it is based. A still life of flowers or fruit, reproduced so much like reality as to elicit comment of that nature, would hence fail to qualify as a real work of art, since it would be regarded as a substitute object for the thing itself—a cleverly attained illusion. The purely associative content would be uppermost in the reaction of the observer—not an exercise of pleasurable appreciation of skill, attainment of aesthetic qualities, or expressive character as reviewed earlier.

Defenders of illusionism would argue that a naturalistic rendering *could* contain aesthetic properties and that, furthermore, in painting the human figure, abstract emotional states *may* also be brought out. The human form may be of no individual in particular but merely a form used as a vehicle to express the emotional state. They would furthermore maintain that if the painting or sculpture expresses some general human virtue, such as justice, mercy, charity, contrition, or hope, it would be attaining an abstract entity. Of course, if this objective were realized, the work would probably not be illusionism or naturalism.

Abstractionism, on the other hand, decries any suggestion of naturalism. The purpose of art should be a search for truth, for permanent values, and for pure form. This attainment would require little or no need for associative content. The forms themselves should speak. There need be no dependence upon regional content, local color, and cultural background for a full appreciation of the art creation. Surface coloring and covering work against the art; the forms should be revealed in their full strength, not concealed. Nor can this be attained, the proponent of abstractionism would hold, merely by a thoroughgoing knowledge of anatomy. A figure rendered in complete regard to anatomical structure may still lack dynamic properties so much desired in effective art.

Hence the interest shifts to the possibility of expressing *forces* by 'thrusts' and 'counterthrusts,' by 'force lines' and 'tensions.' One is here dealing with *power*, with suggested movement and pressures. Art of almost any age may disclose instances of forces captured by the artist. Even works at first glance appearing static may on study be found to exhibit a perfect *balance* of forces: thrusts and balancing counterthrusts, tensions between masses and interests of varying magnitudes so placed as to 'move' in a 'closed' design and with a satisfying equilibrium.

Achievements such as these deserve high praise. They may be and probably are in most instances good works of art. It is highly improbable, however, that their value lies in their abstract character alone. The 'forces' providing dynamic qualities may be resolved essentially into involved phases of rhythm, dominance, sequence, and balance. The abstract character of the forms may even aid comprehension and appreciation through simplification. In most cases the design results from arduous study and planning.

It is in point to note that the abstractionist ideal may lead the devotee into the very error he wants most of all to avoid. In his search for the 'pure form' he may become introvertive to the end that he realizes simply *his own conception* of pure form. Instead of attaining the general or the universal, he attains the particular: his work, then, is the one that needs the guidebook or the diagram. Although perhaps flawless in technical execution the forms themselves fail to call out any real general truth or universal quality. If there is any response at all it will probably be limited to the artist himself and a few friends who have been initiated into the workings of the artist's mind.

It may be postulated that the successful abstract work be *reasonably within fairly common human experience*, but this stipulation does not require that it have simple associative content. But it may be expected that it have *aesthetic qualities* in some manner, form, or degree. A cubist design[1] may supply facets of color and texture in a design that affords excellent color balance, textural harmony, and perfect unity. No one would rule out a high-grade Persian rug or a Chinese vase or rug, simply on the ground that the associative content is not clear. Yet, in these instances, our pleasure in contemplation may be assignable to aesthetic qualities of a rather simple type.

It is unnecessary to restrict the term abstract to blocklike figures and 'mechanical-man' creations or to approximations of objects reduced to essential form. Many assumptions of abstract are more properly *merely tendencies toward simplification*.

Recurrent waves of interest in stylization, embracing both obvious reduction of form to bare suggestion and clever devising of simulated constructs, have also drawn the label of

---

[1] *Cf.* Lyonel Feininger, *Gelmeroda III.* Unfortunately the monochromatic reproduction (Fig. 27) does not provide an adequate conception of the excellent color and textural qualities in the original.

abstractions. In some instances these have conveyed properties by the expedient of suggesting speed or hilarity on the pattern of the slanting line. Others have rested upon established stereotypes. Instances of highly successful creations have used

FIG. 27. Lyonel Feininger, *Gelmeroda III*. *By permission of the painter.*

well-known folk stereotypes so manipulated as to express widely recognized embodiments of political, social, or religious intolerance. In these instances the picture may be simple, abstract in nature, yet with high associative content—but associative content of a general nature. The crux of the matter is not abstract *or* naturalistic. The product can be abstract to a degree and have a measure of general associative content making for better appreciation of the abstract aspect. It must, at all odds, be skillfully done; *and if well done*, in a full sense, it will exhibit aesthetic qualities that transcend other considerations.

12. SUMMARY

In the perspective of time, quality in art touches upon two fundamental aspects: objective structure and consistencies in human response. The objective structure does not materially change. The prehistoric cave drawings, the Ming Period vase, the Greek sculptures, Michelangelo figures—these remain as objects of art from generation to generation, century to century.

The realm of variation lies in man. Individuals exhibit variation in evaluative behavior from time to time. Yet, even in these precincts, change in the fundamental bases of evaluation is not considerable. In fact, there is consistency to a surprising extent, and in this consistency lies the crucial evidence for and criteria of value in art.

The basic feeling states involved in aesthetic response, moreover, were essentially outgrowths of consistent experience with normality as contrasted with abnormality in nature and in man. Balance was normal, satisfying, reassuring. Unbalance was abnormal, disturbing, a cause of uneasiness or even of concern. In pictorial art, literature and forensics, music, or drama, the ordered, contrasted, organized presentation challenged attention, whereas the confused statement, the rambling argument, the unmatched measure, or the non-climactic drama failed to please or merely produced annoyance. Whereas arhythm has been tolerated, even welcomed, by jaded individuals as an escape from satiety, the more frequent and consistent acclaim has gone to the magnificent rhythms and harmonies of masterworks in graphic arts and in music, which today are as much celebrated as at any time, despite some alleged exceptions, explainable in other ways. Generally considered, experience with rhythmic regularity resulted in a feeling of well-being, whereas with unpredictable sequences man was perplexed or annoyed, and more solid enjoyment, more real satisfaction, was derived from harmonious relations; less from the incongruous or discordant.

Balance, rhythm, sequence, harmony, unity, and fitness are simply terms belatedly brought forth to describe qualities in and characteristics of aesthetic structure. When intelligently and effectively used, they produce or effect the structural excellence inherent in the art object and explain the attendant satisfaction in contemplation. They constitute the most universal, significant, and dependable single criterion of value in art.

Deeply intrenched in man himself is a second aspect of art value: the quest for perfection. Practically considered, this is simply the striving for approximations to complete unity. If it is assumed that unity, harmony, and fitness are the supreme attributes of good art—the masterpiece—then universal admiration and acclaim goes to the product that exhibits evidence of intelligent planning, fitness of materials, and skillful handling. Considered broadly it is but a phase of the universal interest in good workmanship, acts of skill, and high-level achievement generally. Good balance, rhythmic relationships, and ordered construction merely describe such achievement in their separate (but integrated) aspects. Skillful execution of the means and materials of production and realization of art principles inherent in the cohering total effects are one and the same in attainment.

These, then—consummate skill in achievement and resultant residual qualities of the structure—make art. In regard to these two vital facts the experience of mankind has been consistent. Man of today can and does appreciate the achievement of the long extinct cave man. The increasing complexity of the materials dealt with, the ever-widening range of man's art interests, and the constant improvement in tools and methods has not essentially altered this basic character of art.

Unquestionably developments have occurred that have superficially at least required new viewpoints. These will be examined in the following section. Without doubt additional factors need be taken into account. Some are perhaps important, possibly significant. But it is at least debatable that they alter the *basic* facts of all art.

Additional increments of satisfaction come from sources other than aesthetic structure and attainment of unity. Some human experiences are more vital, moving, and important—at least to some individuals, and to some individuals during certain periods of time or in certain regions. Some projects offer greater challenge to the ingenuity of the artist; some touch upon wider areas of human experience. So conceived they may be regarded as being interpretations of significant 'trends' or of vital human interests of the group. They may be said to 'express' a deep and readily recognized emotion. They may interpret 'life': human joys and sorrows. Yet in the last analysis this added increment will probably survive or perish as a work of art only if it *also* exhibits good aesthetic structure and consummate skill in handling. Otherwise it must be admitted that a good photograph or accurate sketch will record the anguish, the riot, the dispossession, the evangelist, or what not, equally well—perhaps even better.

In like manner variations and modifications in basic techniques may very well supply an added increment of enjoyment through making possible more ready comprehension. All efforts directed toward simplification move toward this end. Abstractionism, so called, tends to eliminate unnecessary detail and to feature basic, not superficial, form. Tendencies toward simplification may concern themselves not only with design but with line, color, and form without reference to complexity of the problem or character of subject matter.

Art in Human Affairs

Even in these respects, however, the work will be evaluated permanently on the basis of intelligent conception, skillful handling, and attainment of unity.

BIBLIOGRAPHY

ABELL, W. *Representation and Form.* New York: Scribner, 1936.

BARNES, A. *The Art in Painting.* New York: Harcourt, 1928, 2d ed.

BATCHELDER, E. *Design in Theory and Practice.* New York: Macmillan, 1924.

BELL, C. *Art.* New York: Stokes, 1928.

BIRKHOFF, G. *Aesthetic Measure.* Cambridge: Harvard University Press, 1933.

BULLEY, M. *Pictures and Painters.* New York: Dutton, 1927.

CARR, H. A. *Introduction to Space Perception.* New York: Longmans, 1935.

CHANDLER, A. R. *Beauty and Human Nature.* New York: Appleton-Century, 1934.

COLLINGWOOD, R. *The Principles of Art.* New York, Oxford: Clarendon Press, 1938.

COLLINS, M., and O. RILEY. *Art Appreciation.* New York: Harcourt, 1933.

DEWEY, J. *Art as Experience.* New York: Minton, Balch, 1934.

DOERNER, Max. *The Materials of the Artist.* Trans. by E. Neuhaus. New York: Harcourt, 1934.

DOW, A. *Composition.* Garden City: Doubleday, Page, 1931.

FLACCUS, L. W. *The Spirit and Substance of Art.* New York: Crofts, 1931.

FRY, R. E. *Vision and Design.* New York: Brentano's, 1924.

GARDNER, H. *Understanding the Arts.* New York: Harcourt, 1932.

GOLDSTEIN, H., and V. GOLDSTEIN. *Art in Every Day Life.* New York: Macmillan, 1932, rev. ed.

GORDON, K. *Esthetics.* New York: Holt, 1909.

GUILFORD, J., and R. GUILFORD. "A Prognostic Test for Students in Design." *J. Appl. Psych.*, 1931, 15, 335–345.

HAMBIDGE, J. *Practical Applications of Dynamic Symmetry.* New Haven: Yale University Press, 1932.

HAMBIDGE, J. *The Elements of Dynamic Symmetry*. New York: Brentano's, 1926.

HARRISON, H. W. *The Theory of Pictorial Art*. London: Pitman, 1931.

HILDEBRAND, A. *The Problem of Form*. Trans. by M. Meyer and R. Ogburn. New York: Stechert, 1907.

KATZ, D. *The World of Colour*. London: Routledge, 1935.

KOFFKA, K. *Principles of Gestalt Psychology*. New York: Harcourt, 1935.

LANGFELD, H. *The Aesthetic Attitude*. New York: Harcourt, 1920.

LUCKIESH, M. *Color and Its Applications*. New York: Van Nostrand, 1931.

LUCKIESH, M. *Seeing and Human Welfare*. Baltimore: Williams & Wilkins, 1934.

LUCKIESH, M. *Visual Illusions and Their Applications*. New York: Van Nostrand, 1922.

LUNDHOLM, H. "The Affective Tone of Lines: Experimental Researches," *Psychol. Rev.*, 1921, 28, 43–60.

McMAHON, A. PHILIP. *The Art of Enjoying Art*. New York: McGraw-Hill, 1938.

MEIER, N. C. (ed.). Studies in the Psychology of Art, Vol. I. *Psychol. Monogr.*, 1933, 45, No. 200.

OGDEN, R. M. *The Psychology of Art*. New York: Scribner, 1938.

PARKER, DeW. *The Principles of Aesthetics*. Boston: Silver, Burdett, 1920.

PARSONS, J. *An Introduction to the Study of Color Vision*. Cambridge: Cambridge University Press, 1924, 2d ed.

PEARSON, R. *Experiencing Pictures*. New York: Brewer, Warren & Putnam, 1932.

POFFENBERGER, A. T., and B. E. BARROWS. "The Feeling Value of Lines," *J. Appl. Psychol.*, 1924, 8, 187–205.

POORE, H. R. *Art Principles in Practice*. New York: Putnam, 1930.

PRALL, D. *Aesthetic Judgment*. New York: Crowell, 1929.

PRALL, D. *Aesthetic Analysis*. New York: Crowell, 1936.

READ, H. *The Anatomy of Art*. New York: Dodd, Mead, 1932.

READ, H. *Art and Society*. New York: Macmillan, 1937.

Roos, F. J., Jr. *An Illustrated Handbook of Art History.* New York: Macmillan, 1937.

Ross, D. *A Theory of Pure Design.* Boston: Houghton Mifflin, 1933.

Ruch, F. *Psychology and Life.* Chicago: Scott, Foresman, 1937, Chap. 14.

Ruckstull, F. W. *Great Works of Art and What Makes Them Great.* Garden City: Garden City Publishing Company, 1925.

Schneider, E. *Aesthetic Motive.* New York: Macmillan, 1939.

Selden, S. *The Stage in Action.* New York: Crofts, 1941.

Torossian, Aram. *A Guide to Aesthetics.* Stanford University: Stanford University Press, 1937.

Whitford, W. C. (ed.). *Report of Committee on Terminology, Federated Council on Art Education.* Boston: Berkeley Press, 1929.

Chapter 3 · EXPERIMENTAL (MODERN) ART

1. Contemporary Art as the Laboratory of Art in General

Any living artist has opportunity to enjoy a heritage of experience amassed by his predecessors. By study of the methods, products, and philosophies of artists living in the past, he may profit immeasurably. He may then choose to follow one of the models set by some successful painter, living or dead: fashioning his product after the manner, perhaps, of Franz Hals, or he may derive suggestions from Titian, or he may find in the technique of El Greco something that appeals to him even more powerfully. But it is also possible that other contemporary painters will not be satisfied with any particular art of the past and that still others may find good suggestions from many styles. But the problem of everyone then becomes that of developing an individual style— either mainly his own or containing some element from a number of painters' styles.

If the painter attempts experimentally to step out from the traditional paths and break new ground, and the resultant work attracts the favorable attention and approbation of others, a new movement is launched. Such sustained interest in particular methods and objectives has given the world Impressionism, Futurism, and other so-called modern trends.

The artist who leaves traditional ways and tries out variations or radically different methods is an experimentalist comparable to the laboratory scientist: he is working on the frontiers of artistic progress. As in the case with the scientist who finds many of his ventures in the end abortive, so also the artist finds that many of his ideas prove to be vain. But similarly, the frontiers of artistic progress are pushed a little farther out when the movement results in wide acceptance and effects some influence upon the trends of art in general. It is in that way that art flourishes, bringing about new, better, or more effective types of pictorial expression.

Modern art may be regarded as manifestations of change in the field of art, comparable to the experimental phase of trial and error in the laboratory of science. It will be our purpose in considering these movements to enter sympathetically into the aims and objectives of the men who are conducting the experiments, who are trying different means and methods. It will be our intention first *to understand them* from the point of view of their objectives and secondly *to examine them* in the light of psychological premises with a view toward appraisal on the basis of their probable permanent contribution to art. Some of these movements have practically disappeared; it will be our purpose to discover why the movements apparently were unsound. Other movements continue to some extent after twenty or more years of competition with other art developments: it will, in those instances, be our objective to discover what in those movements appears to have contributed to progress in art.

For the most part, the men who furthered these movements were men of high integrity, seriously interested in the advancement of art. One may not agree with them; the least, however, that the world can do is to attempt sincerely to understand them.

In treatment of contemporary or modern art, we shall consider any art developed within the past one hundred years. It will be understood that although beginnings of these movements are indicated, few contemporary trends have definite beginnings or endings—they gradually emerge and become popular for a time and as gradually subside, unless there appears some feature of particularly worthy character. Each movement, furthermore, has its charter member adherents and its normal expression as well as its radical adherents and its unusual forms. We shall be concerned primarily with the typical forms and with the generally understood products made by the recognized leaders.

2. Movements Concerned Chiefly with Composition and Technique

A. Impressionism. Although Impressionism appears over a period of well over half a century and assumes various forms, its essential character is found in simplification. Where it concerns landscape the interest is twofold. It primarily attempts to paint only a simplified vista or scene from a single point of view.[1] Secondly, it features a color treatment of atmosphere intervening between the objects and the observer. The work of Claude Monet, with whose name early Impressionism is most usually associated, dwelt intensively upon the painting of atmospheric and lighting effects. Monet was primarily concerned with painting the fleeting atmospheric conditions surrounding any scene. According to his point of view, it would be possible to paint a haystack at early morning,

---

[1] Reputedly, several movements in art were suggested by a superficial contact with some science. In the instance of Impressionism the idea grew from the knowledge that physiology and psychology teach that foveal vision is the more important aspect of vision—that one sees only a restricted portion of the field at any one moment, the peripheral area being indistinct. To all contiguous areas one must shift his attention. Why then try the panorama, the Impressionist would argue, when the eye sees only a single unitary impression?

noon, early evening, or at any time between and have a distinctly different picture every time. His *Waterloo Bridge* is a painting of light reflections and vague suggestions of solid forms. The effect for the observer is that of a foggy or misty morning with slight suggestions of activity characteristic of the spot. The Impressionists have borrowed from the practices of the Luminists and have made use of color spotting, sometimes with the view toward simply getting a wealth of brilliant color into the atmosphere or utilizing the optical mixture of pure color spots placed in juxtaposition on the canvas. The later type of approach was experimented with by the Pissarro brothers, resulting in some brilliant countryside landscapes. Monet's *Gare St. Lazare* likewise attempts a brilliance in color and at the same time provides the spectator with a vivid impression of hissing steam, shifting locomotives, and a bustle of activity, although he does not employ the true Luminist technique.

Critics of this type of Impressionism have argued that the Monet landscapes have the appearance of flimsiness and therefore lack any lasting appeal based upon the arrangement of forms. They are also assumed to be superficial and incidental treatments, having interest only to the painter who happened to experience the setting at the time it was present. The landscapes of Monet and of the Pissarro brothers will probably stand or fall upon their excellence in compositional and technical qualities. The *Gare St. Lazare* is certainly plentifully endowed with various aesthetic qualities, although lacking in others. The Pissarro type of landscape is designed to reflect light and color to a high degree.

If we turn to a different type of Impressionism—that of *genre* painting, we find in the work of Degas the attempt to achieve a single, unitary, close-up of a figure or activity. Degas's depictions of the ballet dancers or of types such as laundrywomen were accomplished by subordinating the background and all other nonessentials and by a strict concentration upon the theme of the painting. This approach is characteristic of the earliest decades of Impressionism, which held that normal human vision should be taken into account,

Fig. 28. Monet, *Gare St. Lazare. Courtesy of Braun & Cie, Paris—New York.*

attention being focused upon the theme at hand (the act of the dancer—poised, suspended motion) with more or less vaguely sensed surroundings. Accordingly, kaleidoscopic views were strictly avoided—since to see landscape or ballet completely, one must move about—a process similar to the inspection of a large number of individual pictures. Degas's Impressionism, therefore, sought to restore the conditions of normal vision and create the exact naturalism of a given scene or a given situation. Impressionism is concerned, therefore, with the temporal aspect of subject matter. To paint nature, one needs either to paint the scene quickly on the spot or to

return the next day at the same hour when conditions presumably would be similar.

Renoir was influenced by the Impressionists' dicta, since
many of his compositions appear to be personal impressions

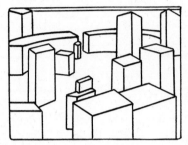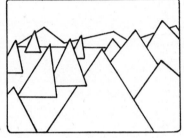

Fig. 29. Diagram of volume organization (left) and of planes organization
(right) of Renoir's *Café de la Galette.*

of scenes or subjects. He went much further, however, in that
he attempted successfully to attain many excellent color
qualities that place his pictures somewhat apart from the
more or less superficial effects obtained as a result of a strict
following of Impressionism. Renoir introduced fine textures
and jewel-like qualities in his painting so that many of his
pictures today are superb examples of color texture and
quality. Renoir also is reputed for his advanced study of
compositional requirements. His *Café de la Galette* is a masterpiece of three-dimensional arrangement. He has successfully
maneuvered fifty people or more into an arrangement in
which they function as effective parts. By a remarkable system
of grouping, he has attempted a unity where there is not even
the slightest confusion or any lack of harmonious placement
around the arrangement. Structurally, the picture may be
resolved into an arrangement of vertical planes placed in a
definite pattern on the horizontal field. If one pictured the
figures and other objects as occupying the space inside a solid
of about the same dimensions, he would see how the groupings
tend to relate themselves one to another and to the entire

PLATE I

Renoir, *Café de la Galette. Courtesy of Braun & Cie, Paris—New York.*

ensemble. These diagrammatic analyses are shown in Fig. 29.[1] Whether or not Renoir *consciously* planned his picture on the basis of the analyses shown is of course a matter that cannot be determined, but it is obvious that the picture is apparently organized in such a masterly manner that the observer is never confused or at a loss to appreciate easily and completely the complicated assemblage shown there.

Édouard Manet also pursued the objective of reducing his compositional subject matter to the lowest possible effective terms. His handling assumed at least two forms—one, the tilted perspective in which he sought a position above and directly in front of, for instance, a breakfast group or other objects of his painting interest; the other being a ruthless elimination of unnecessary detail. In his *Execution of Maximilian* he has placed a soldier prominently in the immediate foreground. The other members of the firing squad are subordinated, and the left side of the picture is given over almost completely to dramatic placement and posture of the emperor, who has an expression of resignation that is remarkably effective. The effect of this arrangement is to make the execution prominent by featuring the brutality of the scene. The same event painted by Goya includes spectators, the mountainside, the distant city, and various contours of the victims. The picture does not, therefore, strike with the same forcefulness characteristic of the Manet, nor does it leave the observer as emotionally impressed. Manet also has made effective use of heavy black outline to make a figure striking, as in his *Boy with the Fife*, and has introduced *black* in his scheme in order to accentuate other values and to carry out his individual style.

B. Movements Concerned with a More Effective Use of Pigments: Luminism, Pointillism, and Divisionism. Impressionism merged

---

[1] These analyses were made by Marguerite Birch Clair, while she was serving as research assistant to the author.

almost imperceptibly into modified forms and new movements. The men who did Impressionist canvases found
themselves drawn to new interests; some to quite different
expressions, as they realized limitations and shortcomings in
their previous work. Hence arose Neoimpressionism. Others
experimented with means for rendering Impressionism more
effective. Camille Pissarro, classified generally as an Impressionist, experimented with Luminism, an effort to utilize
color in its pure form and secure intermediate colors by an
optical rather than a pigmental fusion.[1]

In Luminism we have another instance of the painter taking
his cue from science. Learning that the psychologists and
physiologists regard color sensation as a retinal response to
light waves, each of the spectrum colors having a definite
wave length of known frequency, the Luminists decided that
they would use only those colors corresponding to a definite
wave frequency; and if a color was desired that was not available in pure form, they would get the effect of color by placing
on the canvas in juxtaposition the available pigments that,
when the light wave from them fused retinally, would produce
the desired color in the spectator's vision. For example, a
certain purple could be obtained by placing on the canvas
small dots of ultramarine and rose madder. The degree of
richness could be varied by varying the proportions of dots.
From a distance of six feet or more, these points of pure color
would fuse into a brilliant purple. Or, a particular yellow
green would be secured by so many points of cadmium yellow
and fewer points of ultramarine.

The Luminist attains at the expense of much labor and
painstaking zeal a product that only in relatively few instances

---

[1] The experience of seeing color rests physiologically upon a process of the wave
frequencies in light differentially affecting the cone receptors (color-sensitive
points) in the retina. Various theories have been advanced regarding the manner
of effecting color vision from this point.

has met with wholehearted acceptance. Seurat's *Ile de la Grande Jatte* and *Une dimanche de la Grande Jatte* and Signac's portrayals of scenes about Marseilles and other harbor and river scenes are best known. Cross and Singer continued the practice. It has not been demonstrated that the technique necessarily produces more effective naturalism or realism than other painters have produced with less laborious techniques, notwithstanding the success of Signac and Seurat in creating striking expressions of brilliant seashores and landscapes and particularly realistic sunlight. Critics of Luminism have pointed out the unreal character, the lack of form, and the confettilike, flimsy substance of many Luminist efforts. Plausibly sound in theory, it is so patently difficult in practice that it normally falls short of fully satisfying anyone.

3. CREATION OF A MORE CONVINCING ILLUSION OF DEPTH: CUBISM

As a movement, Cubism had a relatively short life, but its influence in some form or another is still continuing. Since most of these movements sprang up as a reaction to preceding or contemporary movements, Cubism came into existence as a reaction to the formless character of Impressionism. Cubism was, thus, a movement to bring solidity and permanence into artistic representation. The founders of Cubism strangely enough were not those who seem to have profited most from it; those who did gain from its suggestions, like Cézanne, took from it cues and worked them up in their own way. Reputedly Cubism was conceived from a lecture on *crystallography* in which the artist heard that all primary forms in nature are reducible to only three—the cube, the cone, and the cylinder. All other forms are secondary and therefore of less significance. With this idea to stimulate the imagination the Cubist attempted to reduce ordinary human forms like the head or human body into a composite of primary forms.

Of course, concessions had to be made in the interests of subject matter; also liberties were taken with the original tenet. But it became apparent in time, however, that dynamic human beings could not be frozen into grotesque forms. Subsequently the movement grew less in importance, but not until certain variations had become somewhat current, particularly in France. Braque, who is generally regarded as the founder of Cubism, produced a great many still-life studies made up of the placing of all kinds of materials with different textures within a given frame. This inspired some of the Parisian dilettantes to assemble little clippings of sandpaper, matchbox tops, celluloid, and various other things. Later, some of the painters formulated their own studies first with such materials and then painted them.

It is admitted that a harmonious composition may be derived from base materials and that if one enjoys abstract paintings such a picture would give one satisfaction comparable to a wallpaper, textile, or rug design. If the color, however, is not good and the relationships not harmonious, the picture becomes just another atrocity. It must be understood also that many of these compositions were made by creative geniuses, like Picasso, but only for their own enjoyment and as frank experiments with no thought of producing works of art. It is usually the unthinking admirer who is carried away by a well-meaning, albeit misguided, admiration and enthusiasm. Perhaps in this instance the public's disdain for such creations is amply justified.

Though Cubism itself has practically passed out of existence, it provided suggestions for noncubists. Undoubtedly Cézanne, one of the great experimentalists in art, developed his plastic quality in landscape forms and also in his still life and portraitures from experimental treatments of these forms, guided to some extent by suggestions found in Cubism. In his landscapes, therefore, buildings are stylized and made into abstract forms, trees are also painted as if they were more or less solid shapes. An immediate reaction to this type of technical treatment may be that it has a nonnaturalistic appearance. It is easily seen, however, that although the naturalistic character has been sacrificed Cézanne has attained a tremendous effect of structural unity because every form within the area is related in texture, and structural quality is related to every other form. The attention of the spectator passes easily from tree to plane, to buildings, to foothills, to mountains, and back again. This easy transition is greatly facilitated not only by the structural qualities and texture but by the repetition of color and light-and-dark values and the utilization in effective ways of rhythms and of balance. Cézanne was in revolt against the unstable and characterless paintings of the time. He desired to paint his familiar surroundings, particularly *Mont Ste Victoire*, as they appear in season and out of season devoid of cloud and shadow, fog and rain. He also experimented with sharp edges and simplified contrasts that differed from the usual handling of shadow. His landscapes are not dependent upon aerial or mathematical perspective but upon the placement of planes and the direction of attention that structural lines provided. His values were, therefore, simplified with certain accentuated lines carrying the interest on. His buildings were made almost as if they were adobe structures. His structural organization provided, furthermore, an effective impression of deep space.[1]

4. Attainment of Superior Unity and Effectiveness by Special Techniques: Post-impressionism

From the original interest in Impressionism several independent developments arose, partly as a reaction to the

---

[1] The reader is referred to Cézanne's *Mont Ste Victoire* (original in Metropolitan Museum, excellent color prints available in full size) and his *House on the Hill* and *Railway Cut*. These are also available in excellent color prints.

superficial character of Monet's Impressionism and partly as a desire to attain a more effective art while retaining interest in creating color impressions of nature. Most prominent perhaps in the movement generally known as Post-impressionism are the names of Van Gogh and Gauguin. After an early period of indifferent success, Van Gogh launched a series of paintings using almost pure color applied in a very heavy manner. By using thick paint, he was able to carry out a modeling effect; but more important perhaps is the result, from such handling of paint, of securing a total unity throughout the canvas by maintaining the same general brush-stroke character and the same heavy applications of brilliant color. He, therefore, depended very little if at all upon mathematical perspective and almost not at all upon aerial perspective; instead he organized the picture by means of pigment with some dependence upon line. Even in painting flowers he consistently maintained the heavy brush stroke and thick paint and in some instances painted in his background with a peculiar type of basket-weave, cross-stroke design. In a number of his later compositions he used divided color to enhance the powerful color quality characteristic of his mature work. Only a few of his transition period paintings have a thinly painted surface.

Van Gogh, therefore, secured a powerful Impressionism without permitting the flimsy nebulous aspect to enter: his forms were solid and durable. His harvest-field scenes are heavy with the realism of nature itself. His cypress trees appear to twist upward out of the soil into the warm supporting atmosphere and moisture. In such pictures, Van Gogh achieved not merely a representation of nature but a graphic expression of the *realism* of nature. His cypress tree, or his twisting, waving grain, are symbolic of *growth processes* in nature. In that sense they may be regarded psychologically as art achievements of a very high order.

The effectiveness of Van Gogh is also achieved to some degree by his use of distortion that is not confined to a single figure or the human aspects of his composition but to the entire composition. His swirling, twisting brush stroke carries

Fig. 30. Van Gogh, *Road by the Cypress. Courtesy of the Kroller-Müller Museum, The Hague.*

not only the growth processes in a field of ripened grain but extends also to the tortuous, twisting ruts in the road, to the ambling gait of figures walking along it, to the roughly modeled farmer's cart and home, and to the swirling twisting cloud forms. By such use of expressive representation, harmony in texture, line, and color, the use of paint for modeling effectiveness, and various other accessory technical practices, he has obtained a total impression of remarkably effective unity. The value of his creations is that they are as much a function of the effective unification as they are a display of remarkable color quality.

The productions of Gauguin's ingenuity are likewise brilliant in color as well as organization but partake of a different trend and are based on a wholly different locale. Gauguin is known for his Tahitian creations rather than for his earlier work in France. And although he was influenced no doubt by his contemporaries, particularly the Pointillists, his later production was distinctly his own. In the tropical verdure and brilliant lighting of the South Seas, he found a setting for his exotic canvases that permitted him to utilize the brown-skinned natives, the colorful forest depths, the tinted sandy beaches, and the blue ocean for his own aesthetic purposes. He did not assemble such materials merely for the purposes of affording the western world naturalistic renderings of South Sea Island life nor did he particularly care to interpret in paint the cultural and superstitious beliefs of the South Sea Islanders. His pictures, painted under crude conditions and sometimes on sailcloth or burlap, are masterful studies in design and harmonious color arrangements. He was able to take the rich colorings of nature, modify them to his own purposes, and weave them into a rich tapestrylike design. He was not averse to using distortion when by so doing he secured a better organization of his material. Nor would he feel bound by the nature of the scene from which he secured his original suggestion. He has, for example, introduced in otherwise unfilled space some design motif, detail, or field of color to complete the basic design and balance or coordinate figures or forest-tree forms. Although he may not have attained adequate closure, successful depth or space organization, and other considerations that are frequently regarded as important, Gauguin must rank among the great colorists and weavers of decorative pattern. His better compositions should have definite appeal through their sheer realization of magnificent color harmonies and patternal excellence, regardless of whether the observer knows Tahiti or not.

A third Post-impressionist who departed from standard practices of his time and one who likewise utilized suggestions from tropical nature was Rousseau. His characteristic productions are constructions of stylized forms woven together for the purpose of creating a strong unity through clean-cut treatment. In taking liberty with his materials, he at times introduced a fanciful and idyllic character. Public acceptance of Rousseau's works has been conditioned by inability to regard the picture as an individual treatment of distorted nature, but when this hurdle is surmounted one can hardly fail to appreciate the fine technical quality and successful handling of texture and color that make Rousseau's work take on a character of its own. One need not expect his creations to be strictly delineative of a tropical forest or representative of a particular forest setting. The works of Rousseau should be considered for proper appreciation merely as fanciful constructions apart from subject matter and evaluated entirely on the basis of realization of aesthetic qualities of a semiabstract nature. In the latter sense, they achieve a strong unity through their technical qualities alone. Moreover, one must admire the work through its display of skillful handling, quite apart from associative content. His best efforts remind one of the painstaking achievements of Hals and the present-day meticulous exactitude observable in the work of Grant Wood.

Post-impressionist developments have also taken the direction of employing distortion to convey a more adequate impression of character, social type, or other human qualities. Soutine has particularly used distortion in the way of exaggerating the size and inherent character of hands and fingers to express the quality of age and weather-beaten skin. In other instances he has placed his subject in twisted and warped postures to carry out the idea of ungainliness or age, or played havoc with features of the face in order to obtain various objectives of expression. Picasso has likewise constructed his figures in bizarre postures so as to emphasize an angular frame or to enhance the expression of mood. Modigliani, taking his cue probably from African sculpture, has indulged in distorted body proportions, stylized heads and other members, and has achieved both Negro and oriental character in his figures.

In all instances of Post-impressionism there has been a definite attempt to increase the realism of the impression by one means or another. The essential fact remains, however, that in practically all cases the artist was still dealing directly or indirectly with natural objects and not with an objective structure of his own intellectual construction. If the whole range of possibilities from sheer naturalism to pure abstractionism were considered, Post-impressionism would find its position an intermediate one, with most of the productions nearer naturalism. Objects in nature and people were chiefly the motivating subject matter; the special and effective treatment it received marked the justification for designating it Post-impressionism. The Monet-Degas-Pissarro Impressionism was prevalent; they sought to rectify its weakness and its fault and in the process arrived at a more effective art. That they succeeded in their ambition is now evidenced by the still great interest in Van Gogh, Gauguin, and perhaps several others. Van Gogh is now generally accepted as one of the great colorists of all time, and it is probable that the Tahitian works of Gauguin will occupy permanent space in important museums.

5. Movements of Dynamic Character: Futurism, Simultaneism

To the man on the street any unintelligible work of art is usually labeled 'Futurism.' It is almost needless to point out that the reaction is a mistaken one simply because Futurism is just one form of modern development in art. It is not to be expected that laymen be cognizant of the aims of any phase of modern art—much less those of Futurism. The lay mind has long been accustomed to think of art only in connection with madonna pictures, landscapes, and other museum types: in other words, with static subject matter.

That the artist might try to capture such unorthodox subject matter as emotions, mechanical forces, social movements, or trivia such as a dog running has probably never entered his mind. Yet Futurism has merely attempted to extend the boundaries of art interest to include such types of subject matter. Futurism deals, therefore, simply with graphic constructions designed to cause in the mind of the observer an awareness of some *force* or *energy* in operation. By concentrating upon the characteristic symbols or upon clues to activity presumed to be within the experience of the spectator, he can suggest movement and activity without recourse to a temporal sequence of events. The Futurist, therefore, has attempted such themes as moving dog in leash, the cabaret dance, soldiers marching, a riot, or such a novel theme as *dynamism of an auto.*

Techniques employed by the Futurist have included the use of fragments of the objects that normally characterize the complete object or scene (reminiscent of some aspects of cubism); or it may be a weaving together into a pattern of various partially complete forms that in their aggregate suggest the emotion or dynamic aspect of the situation portrayed. Partial drawings of locomotives, cars, tracks, hissing steam, and persons in various postures such as one might see at a railway station—all of these are woven by color and line into a definite pattern. Such a construction might be a representation of *emotions at parting*, as attempted by Boccioni: likewise the placing together of flares of red and green lights, shadowy forms suggesting patrolmen, others suggesting pedestrians, still others suggesting light filtering down from tall buildings may in the total assembly suggest *city traffic*.

The apparent test of Futurism lies in the ability of the composition to evoke from the general observer those experiences necessary for the proper comprehension of the totality. In the main, there is reasonable belief that the Futurists have failed to win public acceptance. By and large, the products are still frequently regarded as mildly amusing puzzle pictures, since most of them require some explanation or cues to their interpretation or even comprehension.[1] They lie between the semi-abstract utilization of symbols of known social concepts and the other extreme of complete abstraction where only the 'allover design' or patternal qualities may be appreciated.

If it may be accepted that art must touch a responsive chord (common imagery or ideational elements) in a considerable segment of the population, then Futurism perhaps has little future to which it might look forward. Despite this situation, however, there remains as a *possibility* its ultimate acceptance as a legitimate aspiration of art and that such themes as social movements, political conceptions, and the forces of nature might someday be more successfully expressed. If one takes the position, on the other hand, that art need not appeal to the general public, then of course Futurism will enjoy a restricted value to sophisticated devotees. Certainly it may be observed that, with the perfection of the color camera, representations of objects in nature may be mastered to a degree not possible through pigments and canvas, but since the cinema exists only under artificial conditions for the moment it is projected, there is left *the representation of the illusion of movement* and the action of forces as a legitimate but as yet inadequately attained objective for the exponent of Futurism.

---

[1] Experimental evidence for this statement is reported in Studies in the Psychology of Art, Vol. III. *Psychol. Monogr.*, 1939, 51, 88–126 (chapters by McCloy and Meier).

In the hands of other types of experimentalists suggestions afforded by the Futurists may be effectively employed to create action and other dynamic qualities in compositions of various kinds. Ambitious undertakings like metaphysical and

Fig. 31. Russolo, *Revolution. Stoedtner Photograph.*

philosophical truths or generalizations have been attempted in the medium of design and color in a few instances. A conspicuous example, that of Bo-Yin-Ra's[1] *Temple of Eternity,* is reproduced in Plate II. The object of the artist is a presentation of semiabstract symbols of religion in the varied forms it has assumed in the experience of man: sun worship, nature worship, mystic symbols, music, Christianity, and other aspects. These symbols occupy space around the periphery (organ pipes as symbol of religious music; thorns as symbolic of Christ; crystals and cells of nature, etc.); the vaporous middle portion suggests eternity, and the temple is the symbol of religious edifices. The painter has in this manner reviewed perceptually a number of ideological concepts, all related to the theme of religion in general. The intelligence and experience of the spectator are required for a synthesis that is necessary

---

[1] Bo-Yin-Ra is a pseudonym for Joseph Schneiderfranken, Lugano, Switzerland. Reproduction and discussion by permission.

before the full import of the painting is realized. The individual whose religious experience is restricted to dogma would hardly encompass the full significance of the work.

It is admissible that the artist is within his legitimate province in undertaking a graphic exposition, interpretation, and presentation of the more complex aspects of human experience. Conceivably, themes and theses like 'Government,' 'Life Process,' or 'Imperialism' may offer possible inspiration for ambitious artists who are reluctant to regard the horizon of art as limited to reproductions of figures, scenes, and common life experiences. Indeed drama, music, and literature accept no restraining boundaries. But in graphic art, as to some degree in the other arts, public acceptance is the unpredictable factor that acts as a deterrent to serious effort on this little-explored area.

6. Movements Concerned with Subjective States of the Producer: Dada, Surrealism, Expressionism

Among occupations that are nonregimented and likewise not directly concerned with productions of staples for the world market, individualism is most likely to assert itself. When forced by economic necessity or the circumstance of industrial evolution the true artisan chafes under supervision and all manner of restraint on his free exercise of his abilities, desiring always to direct his energies toward the fashioning of the best possible product. Modern conditions do not always permit the master craftsman this liberty. Furthermore, the contemporary cooperative-exchange pecuniary society in which he now lives has left him no alternative between conforming or starving. In consequence, some artists have condescended to paint for the trade, others to divert their skills into commercial outlets and find remunerative satisfaction in illustrating, fashion, and the numerous other varieties of industrial design.

PLATE II

Bo-Yin-Ra, *Temple of Eternity. Courtesy of the painter and Rudolf Lesch Fine Arts, Inc., New York.*

(*Facing page* 108.)

But others have resented the times. They refuse to conform, inviting starvation. Still others, good, bad, and mediocre craftsmen, have constituted a large, discontented, and protesting class who continue to paint as *they* desire, placing the onus of nonacceptance upon a presumed unsympathetic and ignorant public. Among them there are undoubtedly some who possess real ability, but there are also many who would probably fare little better in any other occupation. But this unrest may in particular instances stimulate invention and progress.

It is from this independent, defiant, reclusive section that a movement came into life shortly after the First World War. The name *Dada* was assumed, suggesting partly the nonserious attitude of the world toward it. As in all movements there were included a number of able individuals. In many respects the group disdained the opinion of the world and perhaps in defense sought to poke fun at the world. The more serious devotees attempted graphic satire of the times: its capitalistic insecurity, its social artificiality, its grim posing of forces. Some of the creations, on the other hand, dealt with trivialities.

Dada is related to three other movements that feature the independence and free will of the creative artist. *Expressionism* is the more general movement—it may endure. *Surrealism* and *Superrealism* are the others. Expressionism, as the word itself suggests, takes the position that the best art productivity is that coming from the depths of the individual's own experience or, more properly, his reaction to such experience. The position apparently ignores the logical implication that if literally followed any art product so conceived would be of primary interest to its own creator and to him alone. As a matter of practical fact, though, the Expressionist is saved from this exigency by painting themes that are found not only in his experience but in comparable fashion in the experience of many others. Hence the strong point of *Expressionism* is likewise a cardinal point in the philosophy of *Regionalism*, namely, that by turning his attention to those objects of experience that he meets with most often and in the most effective manner, the artist will, other things being equal, be most successful in handling them.

The second feature of *Expressionism* is freedom from tradition and current practices. The Expressionist may, if he sees some derived benefit, paint in large, crude forms suggestive of children's drawings. If he choses to be diagrammatic or to inform in any manner, that he regards as his prerogative. This license has not deterred contemporary Expressionists from attempting to paint personal experiences—emotional flights, boyhood memories, and the like. No one may question the *right* of the Expressionist to attempt intensely personalized experiences as thematic material for his paintings; when the experience happens to coincide with the general experience of others, a meritorious product may ensue if the quality of the production is reasonably high. But if the inspiration (stimulus from personal experience or memory) is too completely individual, then the product will usually be for the creator's own personal enjoyment. Not many artists can sustain themselves on that type of satisfaction alone, nor will any beneficent government feel constrained to support them. Any venture away from tradition and current ideology assumes a tremendous burden: it says in effect that its point of view is right; that others have been less intelligent in seeing the light. If *Expressionism* be taken to refer merely to an insistence upon accurate experience, individually interpreted, leaving wide options in the matter of development of the experience, and giving due cognizance to the wealth of ideas and suggestions that tradition (conserved experience) offers, then *Expressionism* is sound.

German Expressionism, originating in Munich about 1911, was like some of the other movements—primarily a reaction against Impressionism; using for its source materials suggestions from primitive art and from some of the Post-impressionists, notably Van Gogh, Gauguin, and Cézanne. Hodler and the Norwegian Edvard Munch also had considerable influence upon the directions that German Expressionism took. Another German group, known as Die Brücke, including Schmidt-Rottluff, Pechstein, Nolde, and Otto Mueller, centered about Dresden and featured unnatural color and bold decorative pattern. Most of their work has undergone change showing some compromise with realism, and at times they produced some of the best Expressionist works. Another group, including Franz Marc, Kandinski, and Paul Klee, gave the world a variety of productions, from the lyrical stylized animal studies of Franz Marc to the very colorful abstractions of Kandinski and the semidadaist creations of Klee. Marc's career was cut short by the war, but his limited number of productions have maintained a high standard of quality and are still widely circulated even among public schools in America for their beauty of composition and daring use of color.

Modern science, whether properly understood or misunderstood, has, as was indicated in several instances earlier, provided unwittingly cues which the experimental artist has accepted. Our last movement is traceable to the current interest, now perhaps on the decline, in psychoanalysis, particularly the interest in the subconscious. Freudianism and other types of psychoanalysis made the world dream conscious. Though occurring in a state of unconsciousness (sleep) dreams frequently refer to experiences taking place during conscious periods. In fact, some schools argue, no experience is ever lost (doctrine of conservation), and mental life is theoretically at least one vast continuum. We but need some accidental happening to bring to consciousness some event that occurred in a dream state. Seeing a boy sailing a toy boat revives the dream the young man had the night before, in which he witnessed a huge liner departing and a strikingly beautiful girl waving a handkerchief from the rail. Psychoanalysis might inform the young man that his recent moodiness was really due to the fact that the girl he has been going with for several years has of late seemed bored with his company. The dream was a projection of impending separation and loss.

To the popular mind psychoanalysis made a powerful appeal. With its doctrines of repression, sublimation, forgetting, transfer, and compensation it fascinated the casual reader. Quite an important part of the system was the revelation that the subconscious—not the active, everyday consciousness—was really the more important part of one's personality. In fact, it was accepted as being *the most significant aspect*. It was well-nigh all important.

In this situation the Surrealist appeared, ready to change art overnight to conform to the tenets of science, so conceived. Why should art bother with the trivialities of waking moments when there was the vast, mysterious subconscious to explore? Hence a surprising array of creations followed that puzzled, shocked, or amused an unsympathetic world. In all fairness to the honesty, sincerity, and high principles of the Surrealists, it is impossible to escape the fact that successful art, in the past as in the present, must take society into account. For the phases of psychoanalytic theory delved into (perhaps without adequate foundation in many instances) are probably only occasionally met with by most normal persons. It is not possible, moreover, to escape the human tendency to avoid the unpleasant, the morbid, and the abnormal. Man does not enjoy dwelling upon illnesses, whether physical or mental, nor does he like to have continually thrust into his attention aspects of life that he does not particularly relish.

Under the name of Surrealism there has been no doubt considerable false pretense and downright counterfeiting. Some of these bizarre products were designed primarily to amuse their makers and friends or as jests put out to mystify a gullible public. Some of them are only partly paintings, the rest being made up of miscellaneous trappery pasted cleverly onto the canvas.

7. The Tendency toward Simplification and Abstraction

The perfecting of color photography makes it now possible to produce mechanically compositions of rare beauty. In the Bryce Canyon region of Utah and various other parts of the world the aesthetically sensitive camera artist has obtained from such colorful material remarkable products of visual art quite independent of the painter's canvas. Furthermore, the motion-picture industry, employing superior talent, has produced not only great motion pictures, but also some of the world's great masterpieces of photographic composition. The world's store of artistic creations has been unquestionably enriched through this development.

Cognizant of this situation, some of the younger artists have turned to creative individualism and abstractionism to find a medium and an opportunity for producing works that are still beyond the reach of photographic apparatus. Fortunately this trend has taken a turn that essentially brings it back toward earlier art in that it has been influenced strongly by a desire for simplified treatment of complex subject matter and for a dematerialization both of the human form and of nature. Although the search has in some instances led the aspirant into blind alleys, it has in other instances yielded some praiseworthy compositions. Without apparently realizing its full nature, some have even tried to reduce compositions to a scientific basis in the search for the permanent values in human experience and for geometric sanction for compositions of permanent appeal. Dynamic symmetry has thus been one of the outgrowths of the search for perfect form. Variations of

dynamic symmetry where the objective was to utilize a framework that would tend at least to assure unity has also been
characteristic of similar effort. The interest in simplification
has also spread to architecture, furniture design, and interior
decoration. Simple harmonies, the
use of broad, uncluttered areas,
and the increasing use of straight
line and geometric regularity have
also contributed.

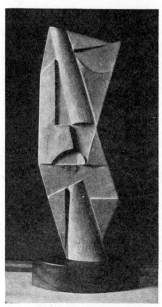

New materials frequently provide new ways of approaching old
problems. Hence the use of tinted
concrete in massive sculpture has
required a somewhat different
conception of form.[1] The experimentation has disclosed not only
that a greater aesthetic effect is
obtained, but that the spectator
arrives at a more adequate perception in an easier manner.
Furthermore, the study of form in
the human figure and in nature has
led to convictions that significant aspects only need treatment,
that the human mind will readily fill in the rest. By omission
of distracting detail and the distortion or exaggeration of a few
very significant features the total effect becomes increasingly
powerful.

Fig. 32. Wilhelm Bodine, *Figure.*

When the process embraces two objectives—namely, that of
featuring significant detail and construction on the basis of
aesthetic principles, even to the extent of employing, additionally, geometric relationships—it has been found that the
aesthetic character has been rendered even more effective

---

[1] For example, Taft's *Black Hawk* on a bluff overlooking the Rock River
valley near Oregon, Ill.

(Fig. 32). Illustrations of it may be accomplished by experiments with simple forms using plastic materials or synthetic stone.[1] It seems unnecessary to assume that a work of art need be wholly abstract to realize its objective. It would rather seem that neither abstract painting nor sculpture nor music need be divorced from some measure of reality. The criterion of value would still rest in the effective manner of use of aesthetic principles, and it is probably nearer the truth to hold that the greater art will be that which has the virtue of simplification rather than the quality of pure abstraction.

8. SUMMARY

'Modern' as a term connoting superiority to 'outmoded' forms is misleading in the sense that art has value independent of time. It is more conducive to an understanding of artistic progress to regard radical phases of contemporary art simply as experimental art. Motivated by enthusiasm and ambition to produce something better, 'Modernism' may or may not lead to progress in art. Time generally sifts out the enduring from the trivial. And in the process it will usually be the effective functioning of aesthetic principles and qualities that will in the end determine the fate of any contemporary work of art— not necessarily any new form, idiom, technique, or philosophy of expression.

Two points of view that express first the positive side of experimental art and second the long-time view in regard to presumed revolutionary movements are presented in the following:

> Social change can spring from a work of art as well as art from social change. It predicts as well as records. The revolution in art is an integral part of the revolution in society, not just a death mask of it. Painting has gone

---

[1] Reproduced by courtesy of Mr. Wilhelm Bodine of Minneapolis, Minn.

through a whole series of revolutions even in the last forty years. This has taken place chiefly in France and is being carried on in America. The current exhibition at the Museum of Modern Art contrasts excellent examples of this period with works by Italian masters of the Renaissance. A great difference is clear, and a great identity is clear in the works of the two periods. We prefer the modern works because they are closer to our daily experience. They were painted by men who lived and who still live, in the revolutionary lights, speeds, and spaces of today, which science and art have made possible.[1]

That statement by Stuart Davis is the point of view of the believer in change. A somewhat different outlook is expressed by Albert Sterner:

Lop off the *r* from *revolution,* and you have *evolution.* Evolution sustains and maintains art. In all the sixty years of my practice I have never seen any revolution in the arts. But I have seen many fashions come and go. In the long, slow evolution of art, in its age-old course, experiments which have taken place, and will take place, all fall into line.

But today it is the fashion to deny fundamental principles in all the arts. It is decreed that competent technique is of little account; that intrinsic beauty of paint on the canvas (oh, there are many kinds) is of no import; that absurd distortions and deformations are the unlimited privilege of the artist; that drawing as it has been known through the ages is useless; that color values build form; that masterly composition is negligible; that only self-expression, the peculiar and particular eccentricity of the artist, is worth while.

To believe that any art or craft may disregard tradition is simply absurd. It is by the handing on of the experiences and discoveries of one generation of workmen to the next

---

[1] This statement by Stuart Davis and the following one by Albert Sterner are quoted from "Is There a Revolution in the Arts?" *Bulletin,* Town Meeting of the Air, Town Hall, New York, N. Y. Columbia University Press, Feb. 19, 1940.

that all art and craft, in fact everything we know, has come about. Evolution, not revolution, sustains and maintains art.

Some art historians claim that environment makes art epochs and their artists. I disagree with that. Whether he is at work on the frieze of the Parthenon or the temples of Egypt and China, or whether, in our own land, he is at work today, wherever he is found, the master artist is in all time an emotional individualist. As such he is ill adapted to any form of collective or union regimentation. Unlike the scientist, the artist neither probes nor proves. He feels. He conceives. He creates. The propagandist themes of racial persecution, capital and labor, squabbling unions, and economic unrest in the world—necessarily and well presented by the cartoonist—are doubtful subject matter for permanent fine art. The cold, mechanistic, pseudo-scientific manifestations, bald, ugly realism, which in recent years have invaded the arts, can bear only sterile fruit in our scheduled lives. For art stands above propaganda. In all periods, as in our own, minor artists make accurate reports of actualities. They are valuable documents. They belong in history. But the great classics in all the arts, the works we cherish and keep, stamped with the hallmark of sifting time, exist by reason of their significant ideas and content, their profound human emotion and adequate technique. They are very rare. The high purpose of all art, of painting, sculpture, music, drama, is by art to express lucidly, to transcribe in some chosen form the vital elements of all nature. Only the poet creates great art —the art that encompasses the mysterious enigma of life, bearing order and serenity into the passing chaos. Lop off the *r* from *revolution*—*evolution* carries on.

BIBLIOGRAPHY

BARNES, A. *The Art in Painting.* New York: Harcourt, 1928, 2d ed.

BRETON, ANDRÉ. *Le Surréalisme et la peinture.* Paris: Gallimard, 1928.

BRETON, ANDRÉ. *Position politique du surréalisme.* Paris: Éditions du Sagittaire, 1935.

CHENEY, SHELDON. *A Primer of Modern Art.* New York: Boni & Liveright, 1924.

CRAVEN, THOMAS. *Modern Art.* New York: Simon & Schuster, 1934.

EARP, THOMAS WADE. *The Modern Movement in Painting.* New York: Studio, 1935.

GASCOYNE, DAVID. *A Short Survey of Surrealism.* London: Cobden-Sanderson, 1936.

GILL, ERIC. *Art and a Changing Civilization.* London: Lane, 1934.

GOLDWATER, R. *Primitivism in Modern Painting.* New York: Harper, 1938.

LANE, JAMES W. *Masters in Modern Art.* Boston: Chapman & Grimes, 1936.

LEVY, JULIEN. *Surrealism.* New York: Black Sun Press, 1936.

LEWISOHN, SAM A. *Painters and Personalities.* New York: Harper, 1937.

MARRIOTT, C. *Modern Movements in Painting.* London: Chapman & Hall, 1920.

MEIER-GRAEFE, JULIUS. *Modern Art.* London: Heinemann, 1908.

NEW YORK MUSEUM OF MODERN ART. *Cubism and Abstract Art.* New York: The Museum of Modern Art, 1936.

NEW YORK MUSEUM OF MODERN ART. *Fantastic Art, Dada, Surrealism.* New York: The Museum of Modern Art, 1936.

OGDEN, R. M. *The Psychology of Art.* New York: Scribner, 1938.

PACH, WALTER. *The Masters of Modern Art.* New York: Huebsch, 1924.

PEVSNER, N. *Pioneers of the Modern Movement.* London: Faber, 1936.

POORE, HENRY R. *Modern Art: Why, What and How?* New York, London: Putnam, 1931.

READ, HERBERT E. *Art Now.* New York: Harcourt, 1933.

READ, HERBERT E. *Surrealism.* London: Faber, 1936.

ROTHSCHILD, E. F. *The Meaning of Unintelligibility in Modern Art.* Chicago: University of Chicago Press, 1934.

SOBY, JAMES T. *After Picasso.* New York: Dodd, Mead, 1935.

SWEENEY, JAMES J. *Plastic Redirections in 20th Century Painting.* Chicago: University of Chicago Press, 1934.

SYMONS, ARTHUR. *From Toulouse Lautrec to Rodin*. London: Lane, 1929.

WALSTON, SIR CHARLES. *Art in the 19th Century*. New York: Macmillan, 1903.

WILENSKI, REGINALD. *The Modern Movement in Art*. New York: Stokes, 1927.

WRIGHT, W. H. *Modern Painting*. New York: Dodd, Mead, 1927.

ZERVOS, CHRISTIAN. *Histoire de l'art contemporain*. Paris: Éditions "Cahiers d'art," 1938.

Chapter 4 · CREATIVE PRODUCTION AND ARTISTIC TALENT

1. THE NATURE OF CREATIVE EXPRESSION

To the popular mind the nature of creative artistic activity is shrouded in considerable mystery. Creative genius is believed to work in a manner that defies analysis and explanation. Even among savants this view is frequently met with and indeed firmly held. The process is further confused by legends and beliefs that have become widespread and persist in the absence of accurate knowledge. Literature, drama, opera, and movies, in their representation of the artist type as a long-haired, dreamy individual who works by fits of inspiration and needs to have beautiful models and a Bohemian atmosphere to do his best work, have done much mischief.[1]

To many readers, no doubt, it will hence seem incredible that some of the foremost producing artists of this age might be mistaken on the street for businessmen or lawyers; and even in the studio it is quite unusual to find them dressed in any manner other than a smock over an ordinary suit of clothes. Some insight into their manner of working would go far to-

---

[1] The word picture painted by Henri Müger in *Scènes de la vie de Bohème* and generations of scene painters and costumers for Puccini's opera, *La Bohème*, have tended to establish the stereotype.

ward destroying the popular aura of mystery that surrounds the artist.

It is of course true that the methods followed by artists are as different as are the artists. Some work directly from nature, painting the scene as nearly as they can immediately from nature, even in some instances completing the picture at one long 'sitting' (Waugh).[1] Others never paint at all until the entire composition is meticuously worked out in a final elaborate working copy that is in turn made up from a half dozen or more preliminary sketches (Wood, Constable). Some secure their inspiration from dreams that in turn reflect in a distorted form previous experiences and contacts (Dali, Chagall). Some get their suggestions on the street, in cafés or night clubs, at teas or dances. Those in the latter class usually carry along a small notebook for the making of numerous sketches as they see characters or scenes that interest them (Benton, Grosz). Others begin their painting at the scene or object, develop some detail with supporting sketches, make a record of the color values, and then construct the picture itself in the studio. Some paint with the model before them and only then; others paint human figures without models; some use models but distort or exaggerate the features for purposes of composition— or expressive significance; others use models but merely for the purpose of building, on the basis of the model, a conception of their own. Some work all daylight hours; some twenty-four to forty-eight hours almost continuously; others work methodically through an eight-hour day. Some take a given landscape setting merely as a basic background, about which they then organize the structural form of composition which, when compared with the original setting, bears little resemblance—and

---

[1] In using painters' names for illustrative purposes it is not assumed that *all* the individual's work follows the characterization. All painters vary their manner, as Waugh depended most upon a trained visual memory of the scene for the actual painting, and others shift to different modes as changes in interest may dictate.

yet the completed composition may be one of extraordinary effectiveness.

Letters by artists, diaries, journals, and interviews with creative artists have yielded a limited amount of information on the problem of creativeness. That there is not very much agreement is indicated in the following quotation from Flaccus.

> A short lyric, a simple bit of music, a sketch may be revealed in a flash in their complete form. They may be made art quickly without thought or the effort of reshaping. Or a line, a rhythm, or a visual image may act as a magnet of form. With a drama or a symphony this is not possible. There elaboration, subconscious nurture, slow and gradual structural building become necessary. This is true also of all but the simplest painting. Franz Marc insists that artists like Mantegna, Bellini, Delacroix, and the architect of the Strasbourg Cathedral constantly and anxiously struggled to achieve form. Of them he says: "That they were artists and knew of art was their blessedness and is mine also; but form was their daily study and their torment. Form is something the good God does not offer us as a gift."

It has been the observation of the author that the working habits of artists[1] as he has been able to observe them have been like the method indicated by Franz Marc.

Modern tendencies have witnessed a liberalization of the conception of art to include not merely painting and sculpture but almost any medium and field of expression. Consequently it is now admitted that artistic productivity *may* conceivably be found in pen-and-ink rendering in illustration, in caricature, and even in the lowly comic-strip panels, for even these require creative thinking, whether the product may or may not attain the status of art.[2]

---

[1] Among others, Hovsep Pushman, Grant Wood, Thomas Benton, Walter Ufer, John Carlson.

[2] The controversial nature of this point need not be amplified, since the interest here is in the mental processes that result in productive work.

Psychologically, the quality of mind that is productive of significant art work is one that is prolific in 'creative imagination.' Though this mental process is poorly understood, it appears in numerous discussions and educational writings. Some hold it to be inborn; others see its development in all children as the objective of art education. To the psychologist, it is a normal and explainable phenomenon, not yet adequately understood but in general character relatively simple. The differences between children who produce interesting and creative types of compositions and children who seldom or never produce work of this kind have been studied by careful scientific procedures.[1] It has been found that the artistically precocious child has probably all the years of his life been much more active visually than his nonartistic companion: he has seen more, he has received more vivid impressions of those things observed, and he has retained more completely all his significantly observed objects and scenes. The distinction is observable in the early years of the ages from two to five and may become decidedly pronounced in the years between six and ten. Hence, when a group of children, some artistically precocious and others artistically disinterested, are all shown for the same length of time, from the same point of view, and under identical circumstances, a four-minute reel of motion pictures depicting fabricated objects and scenes wholly and equally strange to all the children, the artistically competent person has been found to carry away as much as thirty to forty per cent more than the artistically disinterested child. Not only is this characteristic of *immediate* experience, but the difference in amount and vividness has been found to persist for as long as a year. The creative person, therefore, is marked by greater sensitivity to his visual world and by a greater facility in absorbing and by a greater degree of retention. If, in addi-

---

[1] MEIER, N. C. (ed.). Studies in the Psychology of Art, *Psychol. Monogr.*, 1933, 45. Chapters by C. E. Tiebout and V. Grippen.

tion, the personality so endowed exhibits consuming interest in the visual world, a high degree of energy, and some native facility in the easy acquisition of drawing skills, we have the greater and more significant aspects of the creative artist. Interviews with forty artists of prominence disclosed that nearly all of these were engaged in productive artistic effort very early in life, practically all of them before the age of ten.

Psychologically, this means simply that creative imagination basicly rests upon an acquisitive and selective function of a person who is constitutionally adapted to exercise and utilize these functions. Such an individual acquires more perceptual experience than the ordinary individual in a given time and hence, when the drawing situation confronts him, has more from which he can, therefore, draw upon to construct his composition. Additionally, not only does he have more ways of constructing, but he sees more possibilities of *variation* in the planning on paper or canvas. In this manner he arrives at novel presentations successfully with less effort compared to the individual who must proceed from meager material to the formulation of his artistic creation.

Creative imagination resolves itself fundamentally into the process of being able to assemble significant and appropriate elements from a considerable 'storehouse'[1] of graphic imaginal material. For that reason, the cartoonist or comic stripist, in addition to possessing consummate motor skill, is often an individual who mingles freely and widely in society; who knows poor as well as wealthy, successful as well as unsuccessful; he may, moreover, have some conception of economics, sociology, and psychology; he may be more than ordinarily familiar with biblical references, Shakespeare, common proverbs, figures of speech, and fables, likewise being con-

---

[1] In an early period of development of psychology this was referred to as "apperceptional mass."

stantly alert to changes in the social order and to persons about him.

The need for possessing a wide acquaintance with proverbs, scriptural references, common literature, and current attitudes and trends of thinking lies in the fact that the artist, to secure social acceptance of his products, must be cognizant of the receptivity of the public to his conceptions. Particularly is this true in the case of the cartoonist, as an illustration will demonstrate. At the time of the abdication of Edward VIII and the turmoil that the affair caused, the writer appeared unannounced in the studio office of Jay N. Darling, familiarly known as "Ding." After the usual greeting, Mr. Darling remarked, "Do you know the story of Susanna and the Elders?" At the writer's professed failure to recall it, he announced, "That settles it. I'll have to throw the darn thing away." He then explained that he had in mind the construction of a cartoon to be entitled "Susanna and the Elders" in which Mrs. Wally Simpson was to appear as Susanna; the Archbishop of Canterbury, Prime Minister Baldwin, and other English dignitaries were to appear as the Elders. Inasmuch as Mr. Darling had already asked five or six of his friends the same question only to discover that none of them knew the story, he concluded that if we did not he could not expect the general public to appreciate the full point of the cartoon.[1]

The successful creative artist is therefore one who knows the probabilities of his vehicle of expression meeting an understanding on the part of his receptive public. In this respect, cartoonists such as Rollin Kirby, John T. McCutcheon, Edmund Duffy, John Fitzpatrick, and Jay N. Darling have been eminently successful.

---

[1] This incident occurred prior to the publicity attendant the showing of a picture by the same name painted by Thomas Benton and exhibited in the St. Louis Art Museum.

To offer another example, the painting of Grant Wood's entitled *Daughters of Revolution* was found to be the most popular painting in the Century of Progress Exposition at the Art Institute of Chicago in 1934.[1] Mr. Wood had rightly assumed that there were innumerable persons like himself who were to some degree annoyed by the presumed meddling of certain women in national and social affairs without conceivably adequate justification. In the eyes of Grant Wood, simply being a fifth- and sixth-generation descendant of some man who fought in a revolution did not bestow upon present generations the right to criticize contemporaries, who, it happened, were merely tolerant toward a present-day revolution —namely, the Russian revolution. Hence the delicate satire in the title, *Daughters of Revolution*. From the response accorded the picture it must be evident that many people felt on this matter much as did Mr. Wood.

The powerful and expressive satires of Daumier brought out in high relief the social and economic contrasts of his time. This he could not have done had he not been socially minded and highly sensitive to trends and happenings of his time. It is naturally not enough for a person simply to be closely responsive to social conditions; he must at the same time be able to attain a broad and inclusive view, some measure of judicial detachment, and the ability to express this graphically in a way comprehensible to the average person. More than that, he must be able to cast his graphic expression in a manner that will be aesthetically appealing. It is thus not only necessary to be very sensitive to social values and people, but the artist must also be aesthetically sensitive in his ingenuity, which permits him to express his depth of feeling in aesthetically adequate ways.

Considerations such as these make it apparent that the education of the talented child should be directed toward

---

[1] As indicated by requests for reproductions.

making of him a normal, *social* individual and placing him in situations that are likely to afford him a wide range and variety of social experience, a considerable portion of which may possibly be acquired fairly well through reading of books and magazines and attending movies.

2. THE COMPONENTS OF ARTISTIC APTITUDE: MANUAL SKILL

Two facts indicate that artistic aptitude will emerge without stimulation. Interviews and discussions with artists disclosed that practically all of them did drawing, modeling, or painting at early ages. Studies made on very young children demonstrated that the young child who exhibited an interest and ability in drawing or painting during early years persisted in that interest despite occasional lapses through his developmental period.[1] Children who were not interested in art activities when stimulated to the utmost for a period of time achieved commendable work, but when the stimulus was withdrawn the work generally fell off or ceased entirely.

It is probably no accident that artistic ability appears early in life and progresses even without specific training. The explanation is most probably a biological one: the ability, although not inherited in the commonly understood sense, nevertheless probably has an hereditary basis. What the individual does inherit is a genetic constitution or kind of *stock* that makes drawing activities for him much easier than for the person who does not have that kind of inheritance. This is to say that if we have two children—one whose grandparents, great grandparents, and other ancestors worked at occupations such as potters, wood carvers, instrument or watch

[1] The ten-year program of research known as Genetic Studies in Artistic Capacity, conducted at the University of Iowa under the sponsorship of the Spelman Foundation and the Carnegie Foundation for the Advancement of Teaching, 1929–1939. The twenty-unit studies were made under the direction of the writer. See Bibliography.

repairmen, makers of silverware or fine cabinets, and the other child whose ancestors were mainly bankers, merchants, or factory workers, the chances are that the first child would find artistic skills easy for him to acquire, whereas the other would acquire them indifferently or with difficulty. If this situation is explored further, it will usually be found that the ancestors of the first child for ten or more generations lived in parts of the world such as north Italy or the upper Danubian mountain valleys where many of the people commonly work at craftsman activities.[1]

Genetically the process is known as social selection with some of the characteristics of orthogenesis or directional evolution. In such a situation it would frequently happen that the son of one of these families would marry the daughter of another successful craftsman. In such a process of selection the general type of individual whose physical and mental characteristics lend themselves readily to a craftsman type of work would be perpetuated—conceivably even improved. The chances of the less successful marrying thus advantageously would be small in a community where activities needing craftsman skill are the primary activities of the community. Our present-day descendant, therefore, would be an individual who has an above-average number of craftsman ancestors. Actual study[2] of the *known* ancestors of artists and the more apt art students disclosed roughly twice as many ancestors who had followed craftsman activities than others of the same age and economic level. The inheritance factor is simply that *both the present individual and the stock from which he came* have the same

---

[1] Other regions obviously are certain portions of Sweden, the Rhineland region, sections of the British Isles, east-central France, northern and central Italy, certain parts of Jugoslavia, and sections of Japan and China—in fact, any region where craftsman activities have been pursued assiduously over a considerable period of time.

[2] Reported in "Genetic Studies in Artistic Capacity." (Studies in the Psychology of Art-, Vol. III. Meier, N. C., ed.)

general type of build, body structure, and temperamental qualities. These have proved to be the type needed in craftsman production.

Having such an ancestry does not in itself assure one that he can become a successful artist. It means simply that he has the first of six requirements that make for successful artistic attainment. In addition to manual skill or craftsman ability, he must have an average or high degree of *energy output and perseveration* in its discharge. That is to say he must be able to focalize his energies upon a project and persist in it for a reasonable time without tiring or losing interest. Psychologically the trait is known as *drive*. Thirdly, he must have an average or high degree of *general intelligence,*[1] particularly as it is concerned with handling in an effective manner the experiences and impressions that go into an art project. It is conceivable that two individuals may have the same experiences but differ widely in the use they may make of them. A fourth requirement is that of *perceptual facility* reflected in the work habits of the artist type and functioning in looking at, examining, and mental note taking of objects, in a more careful and detailed manner than does the average individual. This is a trait susceptible of considerable training; however, be it noted that, if the person has the craftsman manner to begin with, it usually follows that this craftsman regard for detail will set the pattern of observational habits. A fifth factor is that of *creative imagination,* which we have already discussed, but insofar as it refers to artistic endeavor it means that he must be able to put together his experiences in a clever or ingenious manner so that the ensuing product is one that is effective and appealing not only to himself but to others. His imagination permits him to envisage possibilities that are limited only by the degree of his creative

---

[1] A special form of intelligence which the writer has characterized as aesthetic intelligence is probably more to the point. See Bibliography: Meier, N. C. "Aesthetic Intelligence: Its Nature and Emergence."

capacity. A sixth requirement is that of *aesthetic judgment* which is a process also developed by learning but is at the same time conditioned by the fact that he has the craftsman or workman-like attitude toward that with which he is concerned or about that upon which he may concentrate his energies. Aesthetic judgment refers primarily to the ability to recognize good placements, good arrangements of objects, lines, and colors, in a composition so that when qualities like balance, rhythm, and unity are attained he is cognizant of the effect. Likewise, aesthetic judgment tells the artist when he has failed to attain the semblance of satisfaction that he may crave and what to do about it if he does not secure it with subsequent trials.

3. The Interlinkage of Hereditary and Environmental Factors

In reviewing these six factors it is apparent that the first three—manual skill, energy output and perseveration, and general intelligence *refer primarily to heredity*. There is hence not very much that the individual can do about *acquiring* them. He will normally become aware of possession of them by the *relative ease* with which he can do artistic work and the *relatively rapid acceleration* of progress after he once undertakes such activity. On the other hand, the latter three *refer primarily to learning*, and at least in the case of aesthetic judgment there is no limit or end to the time when he will cease to experience improvement. Even the artist at the age of eighty may be finding better ways and more ingenious procedures to attain unity in his compositions and may still experience dissatisfaction in a dozen different trial compositions.

Considering further the traits dependent largely upon heredity, it should not be assumed that these traits are in any sense inherited but that the individual possessing a high degree of them *is one of a line or strain* of individuals who are so organized that their rapid learning and acquisition of skills takes place with great ease and rapidity. Of course, this statement describes the ideally constituted artistic personality—in America, owing to the fact that the progenitors of most Americans except Indians and Negroes come chiefly from Europe, the actual constitutional inheritance of any one individual usually will exhibit some degree of the conditions described. The fact of its presence, however, is substantiated by several different lines of evidence to which reference has been made. A unique case however tends to offer further substantiation. In the Ozark region of Missouri a boy was born blind and remained so until the age of seven, when he was afforded a measure of vision[1] by a double cataract operation and special glasses. This child then began to paint and draw in a manner that was even better than that of normal children who had had the benefit of vision. A thorough investigation of all the available information proved that only through craftsman ancestry, two cabinetmakers, and a violin repairman, could this phenomenon be explained.

4. ENERGY OUTPUT AND VOLITIONAL PERSEVERATION

In much the same way that people vary in temperament, speed of reactions, and in other ways that persist more or less uniformly throughout life, the artist's method of work requires that he possess certain habits of work that are needed in the production of his exacting and unique tasks. The popular notion of the artist as an emotional worker who proceeds by temperamental spurts and lapses would be difficult to find in actual life among first-class artists. Those who have created the world's great works of art, and those who are now creating works that people look at repeatedly and discuss widely, produced them in a systematic and painstaking fashion. The artist, therefore, represents an individual who elects to work

---

[1] Approximately seventy per cent normal.

out with infinite patience and utmost detail the conception that he has formulated after a period of preliminary study, even though the ensuing product may seem to be in the end very simple in design. Without the ability to work long sustained periods and without the inclination to give a formidable degree of thoroughness to the development of the project there would probably be few great works of art produced.

In the case of contemporary artists some work twelve to fifteen hours a day for weeks at a time almost without interruption. A famous sixty-seven-year-old marine painter works regularly until two in the morning when he has a painting under way. Thomas Benton completed the Indiana murals in six months, divided into a three-month period of research and a period of actual painting of slightly less than three months. The magnitude of this task may be understood when it is realized that the murals covered 240 linear feet of space and were about eight feet in height.

Such indefatigable persistence in the artist is even found frequently in the artistic child who may work for hours on the modeling of some clay object or the drawing or painting of some enterprise when his more easily distracted playmates would be off to several other kinds of activity in the meantime. The craftsman aspect of the inheritance likewise asserts itself in the early adolescent child who works at various kinds of handwork or preparation of specimens for months at a time, the work becoming his most enjoyed and primary interest. Instances could be multiplied not only of the artistically precocious child but of the adult artist to illustrate further the role of perseveration and energy outflow in creative artistic activity.

5. Aesthetic Intelligence

Research extending over a decade at the University of Iowa disclosed a relationship between general intelligence and artistic ability that was apparent from the grade school on through to high school and the adult artist. The conclusion from this study was that higher than average general intelligence seemed to characterize the successful artist. Out of some fifty-one nationally known artists only two showed by a standard test mediocre intelligence—the others were all very superior, superior, or considerably above average.

The component factors of general intelligence are still not well known, but in advanced analyses yet to be made it is to be expected that the artist type will probably disclose superiority in tests involving visualizing, speed in perceiving, and possibly other mental traits.

The Iowa studies also disclosed that among the artistically superior children there were IQs from 111 to 166.[1] As in the case of manual skill and energy, intelligence is a factor which when present with other factors contributes much toward the success of the artist. Alone, however, it means little or nothing, but, when possessed along with high degrees of creative imagination, aesthetic judgment, and other of these factors, it will probably explain the rapidity and accuracy with which the artist develops his themes and profits by his own and others' experiences. It is to be expected, therefore, that the artist having high degrees of the other five traits and a high degree of general intelligence in addition would develop rapidly and would probably progress farther in his eventual development than one without such equipment.

6. Perceptual Facility

By selecting two groups of children, one having demonstrated considerable ability in drawing and other phases of early art activity, the other having indicated almost no interest in such activities at all, and then giving the same series

---

[1] 100 is 'average'; 70 borderline; 140 and above, near genius.

of tests to all the children, it was discovered that in such factors as imagination, recognition memory, form and feature discrimination, and observation with immediate or delayed recall, the artistically proficient group gave much more significant responses.[1] By extending the studies to the sources of ideas that entered into their painting efforts, it was found that the artistically proficient children had much more complete imagery of earlier experiences, such as vacations, ideas of playgrounds, characters in children's stories, and the like, than did the nonartistic. In fact, these differences were marked not only by the adequacy of the drawing or painting but also by the verbal ability of the art group to tell about the painting after it was completed or in process of development.[2]

Additional evidence that the artistic child not only observed scenes, people, and objects more carefully than did other children but that he also retains such imagery for considerable periods of time mostly intact is to be found in the hundreds of children's paintings made from memory experiences traceable to events as much as a year previous to the time the paintings were made.[3]

The trait of perceptual facility hence involves much more than accurate observation of surface likeness; it may go much deeper than that in detecting personality traits, quirks, and idiosyncrasies that usually escape the average person. No doubt the facility is subject to some degree of development through training; the fact, however, that it is observable in the work of children who have not had training of this kind indicates that the basis for it is fundamentally in the craftsman stock from which the individual came. It is, moreover, very likely that the craftsman stock providing the individual as it does with the craftsman attitude of work makes it doubly easy

---

[1] *Genetic Studies in Artistic Capacity*, Bibliography, Vol. I. Chapter by Tiebout.
[2] *Ibid.* Chapter by Grippen, discussed in next section.
[3] *Ibid.* Chapter by Grippen. See Plate IV, facing p. 146.

for such an individual to further his own self-training in habits of careful observation. Work well done affords him with a keen sense of satisfaction, leading to added interest of each future opportunity so that in the end the process becomes cumulative. The writer's discussions with and observations of artists both at work and in other settings indicated that this trait had become very firmly established. In fact, it was the boast of one famous portrait painter that with several social contacts such as eating lunch with, conversing with, or playing golf with a portrait subject he could absorb enough of the person's essential character to be able to paint not a surface likeness of the individual but a portrait that would be expressive of the individual's basic personality. The creative landscape painter whose work commands wide attention is usually the one who after study of the region paints an aesthetic form that is not only pleasingly composed but expresses some characteristic quality or aspect of the region in such manner that the general public can recognize it as such. The process through which this end result is attained involves many accurate and searching observations, the designing of significant aspects, and the elimination of the superficial and nonessential. The still-life painter whose compositions are not merely studio exercises likewise examines a great many objects for the purpose of selecting those that, having significant and appropriate character, may be worked together in a pleasing and effective aesthetic form. The explanation for the phenomenal success of the still-life compositions of painters such as Hovsep Pushman, Emil Carlson, or Chardin is in large measure found in the perceptual adequacy of these men's observations of the materials that go into their still-life paintings and the form qualities that they have in relation to background and other elements. The rather small number of satiric interpretations of human character as found in the works of George Grosz, Daumier, and others is attributable more to the perceptual habits and the uncanny accuracy with which they have been able to 'size up' persons they have observed at social gatherings or in public life and then subsequently to translate these observations into interpretations that bring out the inconsistency in the personality or the intrinsic traits or idiosyncrasies studied. None of these achievements comes by accident; they are a consequence of thoroughly disciplined and effective perception. Once the perceptual facility, resting on a constitutional or genetic basis and amplified greatly by training, is firmly established in the individual it may function in a great variety of situations in the genius type of artist. With others less well endowed it may function in special fields such as portraiture, landscape, still-life, or genre settings.

Some insight into the process is divulged in the autobiographical sketches of Thomas Benton included in his book, *An Artist in America*. Benton has made a number of itinerant excursions through the southern Appalachians, the Tennessee-Georgia-Alabama-Mississippi region, the Ozark country, and the Southwest. Whenever he chanced upon a scene, a bit of local color, a 'character,' or a meeting place of a religious sect, a quick sketch would be made to be added to the rich collection obtained in his various trips. Back in his studio he would organize the material into compositions, model them in clay, make a color sketch, and then paint the picture. Probably little of the original experience is lost in the process. The ability to work in this fashion presupposes a facility for keen observation, imaginatively entering into the personality he is studying (empathy), and of making many subtle observations without obviously appearing to do so.

Perceptual facility is perhaps best illustrated in the following quotation from his book, which gives Benton's impressions of sunrise in the New Mexico plateau country. Anyone who has visited this region and observed the freshness and colorfulness of the desert sunrise can easily appreciate the artist's sensitivity to stimulations such as these.

> The next morning I woke up before dawn. Against the whitish sky to the east a chain of black mountains rose. As the sky turned pink the mountains became blue. There was a bright star hanging in the sky above them. This dawn on the desert was the most beautiful thing I have ever seen. It was moving. It was like the music of some old chant of the early Church, delicate, exquisite, and sad. I walked away from the car. I cherished the sense of great peaceful loneliness the scene gave. I felt like wandering off into the blue, violet, and orange-pink planes that hung in transparent sheets from the top of the sky to within a few yards of my feet. The earth and the sky were as one. There was no distinction between what was solid and what was not. The universe stood revealed to sense as a great harmonious unity, as one thing. . . .
>
> When the sun came over the mountains to the east, the world became what it is. In the place of the one thing there were many things big and little. There were ants at my feet, there were yucca plants and clumps of sparse grass. Way over on the side of a hill, little round bumps of piñon pine squatted in black irregular rows. Beneath another hill about a half mile ahead was a ranch house with a windmill. We felt as if we were utterly removed from the possibility of further contact with civilization. Yet the highway from Albuquerque to Gallup was just the other side of the hill below which the ranch house lay. We found it in fifteen or twenty minutes after we started. Where our trail joined it there was a store and a gas station. The boy in charge there was from Newark, New Jersey. He hated the country.
>
> "This place is too lonely for me," he said. "There ain't a damn thing to see." I judged he had not been up in the dawn of that morning.

7. CREATIVE IMAGINATION

Perception may be regarded as the process determined by previous experience of giving personal interpretation to new stimulations affecting the individual. When the process is self-initiated without the mediacy of a present external stimulus it is known as imagination. A special use of the imagination in which there is an effort to build up a new organization from imaginal content is known as creative imagination. Psychologically the process is not in any sense mysterious or unique.

GENERAL ASPECTS

In the adult world the term has had varied use and with some groups and individuals is almost regarded as a fetish. In progressive education it is held to be a supreme desideratum. It is even regarded as something that every child should be urged to cultivate but with little thought being given to how the end may be brought about. In America particularly and to a large extent in England enthusiastic admirers of Franz Cizek have fallen into the same apparent error into which Cizek in Vienna has himself fallen. It is believed firmly by Cizek and many of his followers that every child has latent talent which, if left to express itself, will reveal the child's powers to himself; that only after that has occurred should teaching be attempted. If he be permitted to study the work of great masters or art generally it is feared he will become a copyist and will not be able to draw from his own experience. Progressive schools in the United States have emphasized, in the writer's estimation unduly, the free thinking and un-hampered activity of the child even to the extent that the teacher becomes practically dissociated from the develop-mental process or at best serves merely as a person to whom appeal may be made on occasion if the child is unable to do anything himself. Tomlinson recognizes the unwisdom of this in the following quotation.[1]

---

[1] TOMLINSON, R. R. (C. G. Holme, ed.). *Picture Making by Children*, New York and London: Studio, 1934, p. 11.

The "give them materials and let them alone" attitude is in fact growing to an alarming extent. I say "alarming" for such a doctrine, driven to a logical conclusion today, may lead to the annihilation of creative ideas. Fortunately the vast majority of teachers are all for preserving what is good in traditional methods, and for keeping a vigilant outlook for any future developments which may seem fruitful.

A modified point of view permits the teacher to aid the child by talking with him and suggesting themes for development from his own experience but leaves the development entirely up to the child. Most of the advocates of this process naïvely assume that the material of creative imagination is somehow existent in every child and that if left to its own devices it will emerge in some manner. There is, of course, basis for such an assumption in that the child does have a gamut of experience that is peculiar to himself, some having more than others; and it is true, furthermore, that the talented child will come forth with many productions without being stimulated to do so. This end will be furthered if those expressions that are natural to childhood are featured.

IMAGINATION IN CHILDREN

It is accepted that children draw most readily and effectively subject matter concerned with vivid experiences within their power to express. But not only is the capacity to experience vividly, but also the power to express conditioned in large measure by the child's craftsman ancestry, which, interworking with environmental opportunities, permits the child to observe more readily, accurately, adequately, and frequently, and hence provides him a sizable stock of ideas from which to work if he feels so inclined. To expect this, on the other hand, of the average child is in most instances merely to invite disappointment.

It has been pointed out that Cizek errs in his assumption that children draw from their own creative imagination. An inspection of the work done by his pupils obviously demonstrates that they have obtained their ideas from well-defined sources—most frequently from the work being done by other children in the group and from the work displayed around the room. Furthermore, the child is effectively taught on occasions when Cizek criticizes an exhibit of their work, at which time the child not only secures new ideas for his subsequent work from examples displayed but also absorbs ways and means of patterning his work from the designs criticized. There is hence a self-perpetuating system that actually limits the imaginative conceptions of the children. Likewise, the progressive education situation merely defeats its own ends to some extent by confining themes and inspiration to the child's limited horizon.

It has been demonstrated in the studies made at Iowa and other places that the children who have traveled or enjoyed wide social experience have the most prolific output, that their imaginative creations are usually of a higher quality, and that the work itself is done in a more advanced manner than is that of children who have not had a comparable range of experience. This situation is of course qualified by the nature of the individual himself. The child who has experienced facile perception based on keen and active observation will inevitably retain more from given experiences than the child who does not have this type of mental organization. Hence, it is all too obvious that two children of high intelligence both traveling widely and visiting art galleries will by no means have comparable creative imagination. The assumption of 'creation out of one's mind' is gratuitous. One does not and cannot construct 'out of' unless some basis for such construction is there. And that can come only from one's experience or, as is usually the case, from composites of diversified experience residing in the form of imagery.

Because the experience of children is usually simple, uncluttered, and vivid, many of their constructions have a charm
and naïveté to adults that the work of older children and adults
does not have. Similarly, in early periods the emotionally
charged but simply experienced observations of a charging or
grazing animal afforded primitive man material for an expressive picture that excites the admiration of modern people.
It is the adequacy of observation in both cases which leads to
the creative expressiveness we now see produced. Had the
child set about to produce a picture of a running deer or
charging buffalo or Santa Claus without adequate experience
he would find it a difficult if not impossible task. Nor is there
much real benefit from having a child draw abstractions 'from
his imagination' of such conceptions as the wind, sound of the
big bass drum, or bottom of the ocean. He would achieve
success only in extremely rare and isolated instances and then
only if it could be traceable to some experience not known to
the teacher, but discoverable perhaps by the psychologist or
psychoanalyst. Creations of this character when probed would
perhaps be found based on storybook illustrations, occasional
looking at pictures in the *National Geographic Magazine* or
Nature Magazine, or probably subconscious ideas—in any
event upon symbols, objects, or other drawings or paintings
seen at some time or place. The adult admiration could be
explained in many instances on the basis of bafflement really
residing in lack of knowledge of the true source of the 'inspiration'; hence, attributing the accomplishment to 'imagination'
is merely wishful thinking, indicative of lack of the true comprehension of the process of creative imagination itself.

The Grippen study of creative imagination is one of few
ever devised to explore the *origins* of creative effort on the part
of very young children (ages five and six). It was made possible
by research funds (Spelman Foundation) and the cooperation
of child psychologists, parents, art specialists, and research
assistants. The procedure was simple. Children were invited,

one at a time, to paint anything they desired at a specially constructed easel. Present unobtrusively with Mrs. Grippen was an expert stenographer. After the child was well along with his 'creation' Mrs. Grippen, who was trained in dramatic and graphic art as well as in child psychology, casually introduced conversation, gradually directed toward uncovering his ideas concerning the inception and development of the 'painting.' The two records, the painting and the notes, were then checked with the source as given by the child, taking the investigator into homes or other places for inspection of books, playthings, home environs, school environs, or eliciting data from parents and other adults regarding episodes and events of the child's past. The process was carried on at intervals and with different children for a two-year period.

A systematic and considerate analysis of the mass of data revealed roughly seven types of creative imagination.

a. From a single memory image a *revised expression* is developed. This category embraces all the more or less simple compositions that are based upon a single dominant object as the central theme, there being added the usual setting, either from imagination or from directly and immediately experienced sense impressions. A picture "Palm Trees" was traced to an illustration of a *single* palm tree in the *National Geographic Magazine.* Two other trees were added and the ground and sky included to complete the composition. Likewise, "Farm Scene" was developed from a dominant element, the windmill, also seen in the same journal. The silo, farm animals, and other details were added to complete the organization to the satisfaction of the child.

b. From several images, usually related, *an organization of the nature of a composite* is developed. In the more intelligent child, art serves the function of aiding in the integration of experience and an organization of the child's world. This type of child is not content to depict a simple object based upon a single image or a simple unitary experience. He will select for his drawing or painting a dominant form that is adaptable to embody significant details or aspects of other related forms. Another and perhaps more common expression involves the grafting onto a basic object relevant and sometimes highly appropriate detail, traceable to related sources but modified by the child to suit the artistic situation before him. Of the former type of imagination the "Ocean Liner" painting is a good example. The dominant form in this instance is the ocean liner, traced to a ten-cent book of ships of all times. This form in itself is well drawn and indicative of the clearness of imagery in the child, yet there is unmistakable evidence that the child also had in mind and incorporated in his painting aspects of the destroyer (mounted guns in the foredeck) and the Mississippi paddle-wheel boat (paddle wheel at rear). It must be considered in passing judgment on the logicality of the last item that the child was pursuing art for his own enjoyment and development, not for adults.

c. From several images *an improvised theme*, resembling the sources more or less, is developed. This type of performance occurred when the child had difficulty in reviving recent imaginal content but finally exhibited something which *in itself* was inadequate. On this beginning he improvised until a reasonable or fairly adequate expression answered. Subject XIB in the composition "Wedding of the Rats" began with a drawing of a trunk. This reminded her of her grandmother's trunk in the attic of her home. Then XIB recalled that there had been a rat in their attic at one time. This, with the memory of a picture of a bride in a current magazine, led to the final composition.

d. From a single memorial experience *selection is made* of various elements of aesthetic interest to the child, to which other elements *are added*. The conditions in this situation are essential to the exercise of creative imagination inasmuch as the

painting itself exhibits little resemblance to the source except-
ing in form. New details, new color (or color where none
existed in the original), or a complete reorganization of the
various elements in the composition have been introduced.

Fig. 33. Source of child's painting illustrated in Plate III. *Courtesy, F. A.
Owen Publishing Company.*

This enlarged graphic conception was not arrived at by chance
additions or rearrangement: it was apparently developed with
due regard for the fitness and function of each new element
and usually resulted in a composition complete in itself. The
conception furthermore frequently assumes aesthetic qualities
comparable to adult standards of excellence. "Teeter Totter"
(Plate III) represents the development in color and design
of an interesting composition from a relatively typical
monochromatic book illustration (Fig. 33) by a five-year-old
subject. The entire work was done by the child alone after she
had, in browsing around in the family book collection, found
this illustration and decided of her own volition to paint
something like it. Two tepee pictures were painted from the
same memory experience, that being an Indian project in the
second grade of the university elementary school. A figure with
drawn bow was taken from an illustration in a child's paper-
bound book. A papoose was added, likewise a tree, from a
source not discovered. The base of the campfire was possibly

PLATE III

"Teeter totter." A product of a five-year-old girl who painted it after having been 'inspired' by the book illustration shown in Fig. 33.

suggested by a detail of the assembly exhibit, but the fire and smoke were the child's own construction, antecedents of which were not discoverable. The papoose was possibly based upon a memory image from some book illustration.

e. From a single memorial experience touching upon some emotional experience a *compositional expression appears as a reaction to both.* A curious caricature, styled "The World with a Cold," by a six-year-old subject was traced to a cartoon by Carey Orr in the *Chicago Tribune*, seen some time prior to the date drawn, and to a scolding given the child that morning by the child's parents for not taking care of his cold. The drawing was made about two hours later when the scolding was still in his mind. Hence the large head (the world) with a cold. The cartoon had showed the world as a head tied around with a handkerchief; this the child omitted but introduced a ring, remembered from pictures of the planets.

f. From a *single vivid aspect of a larger experience* residing in the child as a memorial experience (with intellectual and emotional concomitants), an effective expression, often simple in character through avoidance of detail, appears in appropriate compositional setting. The picture "Lake Okoboji" (Plate IV*a*) was painted about six months after the subject, a six-year-old girl, had witnessed the scene interpreted. This view of the dock at Arnold's Park, Lake Okoboji, in the judgment of visitors to whom it was shown, is strikingly realistic, the child having very successfully caught the dancing waves, tiny rocking sailboat, and the dock. This seems all the more remarkable when it is known that the child's sole contact with the scene depicted was *limited to a single visit*, lasting about two hours, the imaginal basis for this painting being a six-month-old, more or less fleeting, visual image experience while engaged in play with a number of other children. Plate IV*b* is a painting made by another six-year-old child based solely upon a *single travel experience.* The child saw the Rio Grande Canyon while passing through in an automobile sedan en route from Taos to Santa Fe, N. M. The entire trip lasted only a few hours and was made about seven months previous to the painting, which was done in the child's home, entirely as a free volition on the part of the child. Aside from the elementary character of the technique, this picture suggests, with surprising fidelity, the general appearance, coloring, and character of the canyon as seen at the north end (the first part entered, fifteen miles south of Taos). As an interesting commentary of this subject's method of consolidating his experiences and imagery it will be observed that a railway and train appear on the right canyon side. This is the narrow-gauge railway that appears about twenty miles farther down the canyon but is placed in the picture because the child wanted to have the complete experience depicted. This picture demonstrates the astonishing fidelity of imagery in a talented child at the age of six years.

g. From a continuing experience over a limited time interval *significant elements or aspects are fused* into a composition of high character in which form and color are handled in an effective manner. This type of imagination normally is found in the child of above average intelligence who by circumstances of environment or by temperamental inclination lives considerably to himself. In these moments or longer periods the child is receptive to sensory impressions of an intense character which are retained in much of their original state for considerable periods of time. "Summer Shower," by a five-year-old girl, was painted approximately twenty-four hours after she had witnessed the shower from the front vestibule of her home, which is situated on a bluff affording a view of the Iowa River valley. In this composition may be observed turbulent rain clouds, such as accompany brief summer showers, the bluff on the left, and a tree that appears to have been made in lighter value just as one would appear as seen in the rain. Since this picture was constructed not with the scene before the child but

PLATE IV

[a] "Arnold's Park, Lake Okoboji" (age six).

[b] "Rio Grande Canyon" (age six).
Children's paintings indicating high perceptual facility. (a) was painted by a six-year-old girl six months after she had visited briefly at the spot where the experience took place. (b) is a six-year-old child's 'impression' after having traveled through a portion of the Rio Grande Canyon in northern New Mexico. The picture was painted seven months later.

after a lapse of twenty-four hours, and considering the fact that the composition is not photographically realistic (as would be the case if dependence were placed upon true memory images), the example is one of creative imagination of an unusually high order.

FIG. 34. "Comin' Boss." *Courtesy of Carolyn W. Heymans, instructor in the Practice School, State Teachers College, Buffalo, N.Y., and The Studio, Ltd.*

Two curious facts deserve mention. It was found that the more talented children *also* talked more about their productions, suggesting insight into ability to know something of their conception and to verbalize along with the graphic expression. The other discovery was that only in five instances were the productions adjudged as purely imaginative.

An assembly of the art products of children from all parts of the world in 1934 demonstrated that excellent accomplishment may occur in almost any region, with what frequency and under what conditions, however, not being known. Typical of such collections are the types illustrated in Tomlinson's *Picture Making by Children.* Unlike the Grippen collection, which was confined to very young children and the source of which is known, the pictures illustrated in Tomlinson represent work of children of all ages, made under circumstances not stated. Since some of them illustrate inherent expressive qualities and aesthetic qualities of a definitely superior kind one of them is reproduced here. In Fig. 34 ("Comin' Boss") the child artist had evidently observed closely personality characteristics of the type he has expressed, enabling him to distort and 'weight' certain significant parts of the action figure who might well have been the stereotype "Slow-motion Sam." In this instance the child has achieved more than a Negro shuffling along, he has portrayed interpretatively the good-natured character of the shuffling Negro by an exaggeration of the largeness and heaviness of the character's lower extremities in such a way that no one can mistake the heavy tread of the shuffling gait, and no spectator can fail to appreciate the additional appropriateness of the title "Comin' Boss."[1]

BASES OF CREATIVITY

In the adult field as well as in children's work distinctive and appealing compositions are the result of the same general process with slight differences that are not intrinsically important. Generally considered, creative imagination is simply *the process of utilizing sense data recently or remotely experienced in an organization or composition that has aesthetic character.* The process is furthered first by perceptual facility in observing and retaining the experience so that it now becomes available for use, and secondly by skill in the organizing of the data into an aesthetic composition. The process may be rapid, or it may be very laborious. Although it rests fundamentally upon genetic constitution, distinct advantage accrues from training and experience.

That creativity dealing with similar themes may take dissimilar turns is illustrated in Fig. 35. Benton, familiar with the Missouri-Oklahoma-Texas region, has caught the impres-

---

[1] This is the work of a boy who was shy and did not have good muscular coordination, who has since developed a cartoon type of production.

sion one gets while standing along a railway embankment as the train rushes by above him. The closeness of vision and the rapid shift of perspective give the illusion of the boiler's actually projecting ahead. This distortion, together with other angles

FIG. 35. Creativity based upon differing backgrounds and interests. See text. (a) Benton, *Speeding Train. Courtesy of Thomas Benton.* (b) W. L. Greene, *Twentieth Century Limited. Courtesy of New York Central Lines.*

and the smoke stream, creates an effective suggestion of speed. The distortion is based upon the remembered impression and a remembered practice by Benton's father of drawing wheels of a locomotive by a slanting, circular motion, as a survival of earlier writing exercises. The expression of speed in the other picture conforms more to the 'standard' interpretation. One suggests the prairie; the other the industrialized East.

The creative type of artist is not content ordinarily with serving his own personality foibles and idiosyncrasies or with continuing minor variations of a previously acquired formula. Hence the characteristic creative artist engages in activities that are in a large measure original or at least in those that offer some fresh approach. There is therefore a premium placed upon breadth of experience both in knowing his subject matter well and in his thoroughness in working out technical problems concerned with the development of his material into a picture, piece of sculpture, play, or literary or musical composition. Shakespeare could not have produced his many superlative dramas had he not been conversant with the life of his times. Eugene O'Neill in contemporary times learned much in the time spent about the water front of New York City and various other places observing life at all levels. These observations of characters and experiences he attempted to understand better by reference to psychoanalytical literature and psychology. Even a creative composer like Richard Wagner built his great operas from thematic materials gathered from various sources. His operas are not intrinsically unique units each wholly different from others, but on the other hand even the occasional operagoer may detect repeated phrases and borrowings from common sources that appear and reappear even in the same opera. This process of drawing upon the community of music 'source material' discounts in no way the greatness of Wagner as a creative artist but is merely illustrative of the fact that the creative artist draws from the world's stock of ideas, adding perhaps many himself. His genius is as much a matter of knowing what there is in the world from which he may draw as it is in adding original material.

The creative painter who takes for his main interest people and life of his times must necessarily be to some degree *en rapport* with life and societal problems with his interest extending to economic and political problems; it may venture into religious and philosophical conceptions, or it may be concerned primarily with human virtues. Familiar examples of each three types of interest may be seen in the cases of Daumier, Goya, Schneiderfranken (Bo-Yin-Ra), and Titian. In any case these individuals saw mankind with an understanding eye. In the process of creative imagination much human experience and knowledge is given symbolic or generalized expression. In the use of generalization and symbols the artist must utilize his imagination in an additional sense of projecting his thinking into that of the public in order to predict whether or not there is sufficient common experience between himself and the public to permit the public to appreciate his conception.

The dependence of creative imagination upon elements entering into the past experience of the individual is well illustrated in the methods of Hovsep Pushman, who is regarded as one of the great still-life painters of all time. Mr. Pushman has traveled widely and has accumulated an extensive collection of objects of art from various parts of the world but particularly from China, India, and the Near East. This collection in his New York studio constitutes a veritable private museum and includes several hundred frames which are of such variety and character as to make it possible to select one extremely well fitted to the tonal and textural character of the painting. The still life is thus a product of his unerring selection of objects from his museum, his unfailing aesthetic judgment in arranging these objects not only to form a marvelously beautiful composition but also to provide the material basis for a flawlessly painted composition. In the process perceptual facility, creative imagination, and aesthetic judgment function as a unit guided by a superior aesthetic intelligence. There is also present in the situation a constantly high outflow of energy that utilizes superior manual skill.

The interworking of perceptual facility, creative imagination, and aesthetic judgment is perfectly illustrated in the conception, planning, and construction of Grant Wood's *Daughters of Revolution*, referred to previously. Irked by the behavior of some individuals, he seized upon *contrast* as the principle on which to base his satire. Hence the employment of contrast of color and the inclusion of Leutze's *Washington Crossing the Delaware*. It is to be noted that the incentive for this picture was a succession of news items; the creative part wherein imagination functions is in the manner in which Mr. Wood sought out and utilized photographs that would serve as a vehicle for the satire. The three faces in the picture are constructs though based upon a study of many photographs, the actual identity of the persons being unknown. But behind the selection lies Mr. Wood's keen perceptual experiences in observing 'types' such as he now unerringly sought out to serve the purpose of the satire.

The process of creative imagination may be illustrated prolifically by methods followed by painters of other periods. Historical research has painstakingly uncovered source material used by Renaissance painters. Many of the best known classical works may now be shown to have been constructed from 'borrowings' from earlier periods and from reconstructed objects of art—statues, cameo figures—and from the mythology of antiquity. In many instances the specific materials have been located and the likeness noted. The practice in no way detracts from the genius of the painter; the process is inevitable as being simply the way in which the creative mind works, and the 'borrowed' material is seldom slavishly copied but rather reworked to fit more harmoniously into the schema of the composition. Ghiberti was known as a collector of antiques. There is evidence that Michelangelo had occasion to model some of his Vatican figures from cameo figures of the Medici collection.

So much were the borrowings in evidence during the Renaissance that some scholars regard it as a revival of antiquity. Greek civilization was to them what all of European civilization is to us except that it was obviously much circumscribed. A few examples of these borrowings will be cited.[1]

> If we look for one both famous and already sufficiently well explained, none could be found more conspicuous than Botticelli's *Birth of Venus*. It is a painted myth, and an antique one. How Venus emerged from the waves, how the mild winds drove her to the island of Cyprus, who was

---

[1] The author is indebted to Professor Otto Brendel, department of art history at Washington University, St. Louis. The quotations are from an unpublished manuscript, "The Revival of Antiquity in Italian Renaissance Painting."

waiting to receive her, and how flowers grew around her on the barren sea: all this was originally antique poetry, retold in the verses of Poliziano the Florentine, and thus has come to the knowledge of the Florentine painter. A good poetical invention is rarely, if ever, exhausted; it is always a pleasure to retell it. From this point of view, the performance of the painter is based on a more or less literary experience. We could call it a model example of illustration, and illustration indeed is one of the main roads on which antique subjects have made their entrance into modern art and modern thinking in general. But as to Botticelli's painting, this would not cover all. The wandering thoughts of poetry may enter a work of art, as the platonic soul could enter a material body. The primordial material of an artist, however, is not vagrant imagination, but the permanent visibility of form. Now it is obvious and well known that Botticelli has used an antique model even in his figure composition. His Venus herself is derived from a rather common antique representation, the most famous representative of which is the so-called *Venus de Medici* in Florence. This means that an antique statue was introduced with comparatively slight changes into a modern picture. Clearly, in this case the artistic interest is concentrated exactly on what we might call an isolated motive or invention, namely, the interpretation of a human figure in a given situation by a specific posture. It is this posture which has been taken over from the antique prototype. The old invention is used as freely as if it were raw material to be discovered by a knowing eye, unfolding a new charm within the unfamiliar setting of Botticelli's pictorial surroundings. The case of Botticelli's Venus is by no means uncommon, and the revival of certain antique inventions, especially of single figures, must have been much more frequent in Renaissance painting than we still are aware of. It was not even limited to such examples in which an antique subject was rendered but may easily be found in Christian or allegorical compositions as well.

Michelangelo, we are assured by Vasari, thanks to his good memory could avail himself of the works of others

"in such a manner that hardly anyone has ever noticed it."
Considering the extraordinary gift of imagination displayed by this artist, we may at first be even more surprised
to hear that he did avail himself of such works at all. But
if there were any doubt, examples show that Vasari was
right. In fact we could misunderstand what the revival of
antiquity really meant, if we would not believe him. The
more attention we pay to this subject, the more the self-
evidence becomes intelligible by which these artists did
"avail themselves" of classical works. They were dis-
coverers, but as such they were essentially artists, not anti-
quarians. Obviously they admired antique art. But it has to
be said that their admiration was more spontaneous and
less academic than any purely neoclassic imitation of a few
examples would ever be. Quite the contrary, they seem to
have considered the whole of antiquity for the most part as
a natural and inexhaustible source of inspiration. For them
it was like a mine which they exploited freely.

Examples are particularly abundant in Michelangelo's
work. In fact, this seems to hold good for the greater part
of the seated youths, who, in their endless variety, are part
of the architectural arrangement painted on the Sistine
ceiling. One, as has been observed long ago, was taken
over from a gem representing Orpheus. It is probable that
also Titian's Orpheus has something to do with the same
jewel. The influence of such small works reaches very far
sometimes. Especially instructive is the case of those antique gems from the Medici collection which were copies,
and correspondingly enlarged, in a series of *tondi* decorating
the Palazzo Medici-Riccardi at Florence. Among them
was the famous intaglio from the collection of Niccoli, in
which Diomedes is represented robbing the Palladium of
Troy. He raises himself cautiously from the altar. Also his
peculiar posture was used by Michelangelo in the Capella
Sistina. So was the young satyr on the left shoulder of
whom the child Dionysos is riding. Michelangelo had no
use for either the child or the cloth filled with various
fruits; but he took up the inspiration, as still can be noticed
with a beautiful figure on the same ceiling. Perhaps still
wider is the material connected with another one of these

peculiar compositions. It represents Dionysos and a group
of satyrs, all copies from antique motives. The first work
in which one of their motives was recognized again was
Mantegna's Bacchanal with the wine cask. Mantegna
dropped the little Pan supporting the drunk Dionysos and
thus produced a new figure in a very striking position. If
Filippino Lippi had ever finished the allegorical composition which he outlined on his sketch at Oxford, another
copy of the same Dionysos would become apparent. Just
enough is preserved to allow us to make this statement.

Ideas, as every historian knows, usually do not jump out
of human heads, as did Athena from the head of Zeus.
They have a history. Every additional intuition into the
history of an artistic motive will bring about a further
understanding of its inherent beauty, as well as of the full-
ness of imagination proper to the artist who knows how to
make use of it. This is one advantage derived from such
comparisons. The other is that they alone will further our
understanding of what the revival of antiquity really was,
as far as the sheer visibility of artistic forms is concerned.
By these comparisons we may learn how the oft-noticed
ubiquity of antique art was brought about in the works of
Italian Renaissance painters. This fine element may in
certain works seem to be omnipresent like air, but it cannot
well be invisible like air. The impressions of its presence,
wherever it arises, must be based on concrete facts. Very
often these facts will be provided by the better knowledge
of a single motive or a posture, the original of which can be
traced back to a work of antique art. For all Renaissance,
as far as its relation to antiquity is concerned, was nothing
other than an enormous process of reintegration. Hence
the growing richness of ideas, symbols, subjects, and forms
was brought about which we admire as a phenomenon
still unrivaled in the history of art.

8. AESTHETIC JUDGMENT

The two previously reviewed factors, perceptual facility
and creative imagination, represent past and present stages
in the process of creating a work of art. A final factor, aesthetic

judgment—probably the most important single factor in the entire process—refers to critical appraisal of the work in progress or of a completed work of art. Simply defined, aesthetic judgment is the ability to recognize aesthetic quality residing in any relationship of elements within an organization. It is vital to the artist in that good aesthetic judgment permits him to know when it is good or, if it is unsatisfactory, what might be done to improve it. It is also basic to art criticism and underlies the appreciative aspect of aesthetic response. Studies[1] show that it is present in children to some degree, but it is undoubtedly subject to considerable development through learning and experience. It is probably never completely mastered by anyone.

In the interest of clarification it will be understood that aesthetic judgment does not imply the application of a series of rules or maxims. In fact it has little to do with rules; only insofar as it has reference to constants at all does aesthetic judgment refer to the general principles discussed in Chap. 2. But although these constants may usually be in the background of most judgments, the process of judging is primarily an individual matter.

By the same token each person's manner of attaining compositional arrangements involving balance, rhythm, sequence, or unity is always his own—an individual way of arriving at ends that he understands from long experience and training. It is the end result rather than the manner of attainment that provides the basis for agreement, which in turn rests upon constants in human experience. The qualities of effective balance, rhythm, sequence, or the approach to perfect unity excite admiration today as they have in remote periods. Hence the interest is not merely in the attainments; it is also in the *manner* of attainment. In fact, so much is it an individual

---

[1] *Psychol. Monogr.*, 1933. Studies by Daniels, Jasper, Whorley, and Walton.

process that in repeating a compositional study the same individual would probably never duplicate any preceding attainments yet may have secured admirable aesthetic qualities in all of them.

Although it has been found that even small children in some instances disclose by discriminatory responses an awareness of "better than" or "not so good as" in comparison of one design or arrangement with another, and hence suggest some kind of unlearned (formally at least) ability,[1] it is possible that the facts may be accounted for in a way that does not require either learning or heredity alone. Here again we confront the idea of *interlinkage*, where it is well-nigh impossible to determine precisely what is attributable to heredity and what to environment.

In the instance of the child at play with blocks the arranging of the blocks in *orderly patterns* (Czurles) *may* be motivated by an attitudinal disposition adopted by the child from parents. This hypothesis would demand much from a two- or three-year-old child and imply a considerable transfer. Yet it is not beyond the range of probability, though doubtful.

Since we do not accept direct heredity as an explanation, the other possibility would be that of the inheritance of a genetic constitution that makes it simple for the child to engage in activities that express bodily activity patterns. This explanation does not exclude the other; in fact, the two possibilities may function concomitantly, but acceptance of the latter view makes it unnecessary to assume that a child at such an early stage of development would be observant to such a degree of parental or other adult habits and acts.

---

[1] As reported in the previously mentioned studies (Carnegie project) and the intensive case study of Stanley Czurles ("The Emergence of Art Ability in the First Three Years of Life," unpublished master's thesis, Syracuse University, Syracuse, N. Y.).

The author's repeated observations on artists at work and study of their manner of arriving at aesthetic judgments, their habits, tastes, and personalities have tended to confirm the latter point of view. It is hence proposed that there is a hitherto unsuspected relationship between craftsman heredity and the higher degrees of aesthetic judgment constantly in evidence on the part of many artists. *The explanation lies in the manner of work itself.* Viewed in this sense aesthetic judgment is fundamentally referable to pride in orderly arrangement. The true craftsman[1] takes great pride in superlative, not ordinary, achievement; the ideal is always an objective and sought by painstaking endeavor and infinite patience. In the area of artistic striving it takes the form of an engrossing search for perfection. Specifically in the development of a painting the artist adhering to the craftsman ideal will strive for nicely proportioned relationships and good allover design and will make infinite and persistent efforts in the attainment of unity. Indeed, if in the craftsman generally, craftsman nature is such as to demand good workmanship of a physical type, it is reasonable to assume that the same personal concern for orderly arrangement in a painting or a simplified or unified design also characterizes the *mental attitude* of the painter or sculptor.

The parallel is moreover evident in personality aspects of craftsman nature and artistic nature. The latter is notoriously[2] characterized as 'temperamental,' which analyzes usually into *sensitivity* due to his greater keenness of perception and introvertive nature. Like the keen-visioned craftsman or worker in activities requiring fine perceptions, the artist must be able to detect niceties in minutely different relationships. The conse-

---

[1] The reader will observe that "craftsman" refers to a fashioner of any kind of product whether it be jewelry, furniture, or a piece of sculpture or a painting. In the sense here used it connotes special skill and should not be taken to imply a minor form of applied art activity as suggested by the designation "arts and crafts," which frequently limits crafts to minor handwork.

[2] In actuality, however, quite erroneously and inaccurately.

quent habit leading him to see significance in detail which to the layman may appear minor soon tends to brand him as finical. Yet the demands of aesthetic structures make it imperative that he maintain this high standard of perception and judgment. It simply requires greater discernment to plan rhythmic color sequences or intricately balanced masses or harmoniously adjusted size-weight relationships.

The interlinkage of craftsman heredity and the rapid and effective attainment of a greater and greater degree of aesthetic judgment is apparently a matter of interaction. The craftsman manner leads naturally to adoption of practices that in them-selves represent the craftsman *attitude* applied to the work at hand. These practices in turn influence the mental phase of deciding problems of selection and arrangement. Hence the judgment process expands, profiting from the craftsman's own experience and from observations of others when they conform to his craftsman 'sense' of fitness and order.

9. IMPLICATIONS OF THE INTERLINKAGE THEORY

Inasmuch as the theory set forth touches upon the nature-nurture controversy, it is desirable that certain aspects be clearly understood. The writer has long shared the conviction of careful students of this problem that it is as wrong to assume that artists are 'born' as it is that artists are 'made.' Such extreme simplification should not be sought. Neither long study of hereditary charts nor the supposedly rigid control of environmental influences has offered convincing evidence in either case. Nor does it seem profitable to attempt to find which is the more influential of the two.

Evidence accumulated and checked with the current viewpoints of biology indicates that some aspects of artistic capacity are largely attributable to the factor of *stock inheritance*, and others are more attributable to learning; but the point should be emphasized that the hereditary factor referred to is not heredity in the sense of direct inheritance and, furthermore, that the environmental aspect is not environmental influence in the usual sense, but a relationship between the individual and his aesthetically significant environment wherein the *individual himself* takes the initiative. Nature and nurture are here not separate elements, since they do not act directly but interact in a dynamic, total situation. The six factors outlined above are therefore more *a series of conditions which, when present, interact with the energies of the individual to develop his artistic competence.* The individual therefore, not the inheritance or the environment, is the final determiner in the situation. The person may have the constitutional stock in the same manner possessed by a long line of craftsman ancestors, but he may not wish to develop the potential skill present; he may prefer to sell bonds or engage in law practice. He may have the temperamental trait of perseveration with inexhaustible energy reserves; but he may wish to apply it to scientific research. He may have the peculiar perceptual facility that goes with the artist personality; but he may wish to use it for nature study or biological research. The special ability known as artistic capacity refers therefore to developmental potentialities which when used through the volition of the individual lead to extraordinary accomplishment in the area. It devolves upon the individual to bring this about.

It is the thesis of the author that the person with the six factors *can* bring this end about and that the person without these factors *cannot* bring this about to any great degree. Certain neurophysical and developmental factors seem to be normally a *precondition* for the rest of the total development. These predisposing conditions are not present equally in all persons nor can they be established if absent. The factors are not only interlinked in the gross aspects, but they are interlinked and condition one with the other in a dynamic sense, *i.e.*, the interrelationships may change with time and may exist in varying potencies with different individuals. There are probably no two individuals who present identical composites of factors to begin with, and these composites are probably different at each stage of development. It is firmly believed nonetheless that in all cases the *general pattern* is that described above, involving the factors of motor skills, the volitional-temperamental traits of energy output and perseveration, intelligence, habits of perceiving, special utilization of imagination, and a special disciplining of judgment and critical processes. Paradoxical as it may seem, it is yet noteworthy that, although the basic fact remains that artistic capacity rests upon a general stock inheritance, even the *acquired phases* relating to perception, imagination, and judgment are themselves *conditioned by this inheritance*. All these factors are in a peculiar and unique manner *interlinked*, and the entire dynamic process is a closely knit, interdependent, and evolving development.

10. The Psychology of Artistic Invention

The manner in which the conception of a picture, piece of sculpture, or other art creation takes place is no doubt less mysterious to the creative artist than to anyone else. There is of course no stereotyped process. Neither does the artist himself follow a formula or pattern of work consistently—certainly not methodically, although some permit habits of work to become fairly routine. In some instances the procedure has evolved so gradually that the artist is unaware of his various steps in conceiving, planning, and producing the picture. If pressed he could hardly give an adequate explanation. Yet there are others who are fully aware of their work habits and can elucidate them readily.

In order to remove some of the unwarranted aura of mystery from the process in general it may be demonstrated that knowing the background of the artist, his work habits, his life interests, his personality, and his works already accomplished it is not difficult to surmise his probable work practices. Furthermore, knowledge of the traits in artistic talent aid materially in understanding the process of conception of art themes. If the individual's perceptual facility has been applied to marine phenomena, for instance, it would follow that his visual and auditory memory should be highly developed.[1] From these experiences keenly felt at the moment would be preserved material for later composition. Ritschel's *The Derelict* is a good example, Ritschel having seen the ship, which occupies a prominent role in the composition, while sailing in Atlantic waters in the vicinity of the Sargasso Sea. If the dominant interest of the artist should happen to be people, then we should expect the artist to frequent cafés, parks, water fronts, factories, slums, or public buildings, depending upon his particular special interest. At these places of vantage he would not only find the needed perceptual experience but might commonly carry a convenient sketchbook for retaining in more detail the character or scene he had just observed. With the creative artist, however, isolated perceptions seldom suffice for a serious work of art. But the suggestion, rather, that the experience affords is of value for development, for integration, with a previously envisaged setting of social or human significance. Perhaps there had been a half-formed theme in mind for some time; now two characters are seen in a situation that completes the idea for which the artist had been groping. The active serious artist may have several themes in mind for possible future development; some may be resolved by research, by actively seeking in libraries for the needed elements, or by frequenting locales where the types or objects are likely to be found.

---

[1] Waugh, Ritschel, and Daugherty have been close and ardent students of the sea. Ritschel sailed the seas at one time.

In the colorful Southwest the late Walter Ufer utilized frequently two basic materials for his brilliant canvases: the natural settings about Taos, N. M., and one or more Indians with ponies. In practice the setting was first sought (sagebrush-studded plain, arroyo, mountain background), after which the Indians mounted or dismounted were moved about until the ensemble proved satisfactory for the purposes of the composition.[1] This procedure might be styled composing by combining natural elements with manipulation of human interest elements through a shifting about until the desired relationships were arrived at. The actual painting was partly done on the spot and completed in the studio.

A variation of the procedure is followed by a number of painters who feature regional subject matter. Much scouting precedes the selection of locale. A preliminary sketch, or perhaps several, made on the spot, forms the basis for studio development. As the composition takes form the painter may return to the locale for closer study of detail, or the procedure may require that elements found elsewhere may be appropriated for integration into the evolving composition. For just such eventualities the artist may collect and retain sketched items gathered at various times from travels or from visits about the region.

With the still-life painter the procedure is considerably a matter of having access to good, paintable material. Pushman, as an example, had the good fortune to have a veritable private museum, the result of collections from wide travels, from which he could select objects, manipulate them against various harmonized backgrounds, and in the end secure a material basis for his still life. The genius was evinced not alone in the arranging but in the consummate skill in handling of pigments to create from the material a painting of exquisite beauty.

---

[1] As outlined to the author.

The creative genius may function in the absence of material that would ordinarily be stimulating, but the great productions would seem to be a product of having both significant and strongly stimulating *subject matter* (the sea, colorful arid regions, fine *objets d'art*, or striking personalities having wide appeal) and *wide experience* in handling the material. Studies by Dr. Harvey Lehman tend to show that the periods of highest creativity are the ages from thirty-five to forty-five, which in the artist would be that where technical skill would be at its best and contacts with subject-matter possibilities also at a maximum.

11. DESIGN-CREATION PROCEDURES

In art precincts other than the planning and development of great works design takes form in endless ways. In relatively simple design such as textile patterns, even whims may occasionally produce one that enjoys a period of popularity. By the simple expedient of scattering carpet tacks and sugar cubes over a flat surface, creating, by a light from a low point, lengthened shadows in the intervening spaces and photographing from above, the basic pattern may be established. The designer may proceed from a simple theme such as jacks and marbles or pots and pans, stylized for the purpose of welding them together into an allover pattern. These procedures may be called adventitious design, since the elements are selected by accident or whim. Regions of general interest may be taken as a basis. Niagara Falls or the Mexican desert or Polish peasant costume details may find their way into textile print patterns.

Nature is likewise a prolific source of suggestions for design. Flowers, plants, clouds, mountains, and the like have been worked and reworked in the design laboratories and studios. The search for new ideas extends to distant regions when the local ones cease to attract.

Ethnography or the cultural products of peoples offer new interests to the advanced designer. Exploring farther into Mexico and Central America, ancient Aztec and Mayan designs have been called upon to furnish architectural and textile patterns. Chinese and Hindu motifs have had their day also, and more recently Bali and Siam have been visited for dance themes and ideas for graphic design.

A well-known automobile at one time brought out 'period models' in which the exterior color scheme conformed to the predominant or characteristic colors of the period. The textiles used on the seat covers and linings of the sides of the car interior were likewise decorated with the coat of arms of the ruling monarch or the symbol of the period or region. There were included a characteristic pattern and color scheme for a Louis XIV, Elizabethan, and Louis XVI, among others, and a Chinese (dragon motif with black and gold coloring) and, to satisfy the wealthy winter-vacationing class, an 'American' model, featuring a color scheme of 'Miami' orange and Palmetto green. With these elaborate designs, prepared after months of study in the Metropolitan Museum and other repositories of source material, the company could offer to a limited public models to match the customer's home decorative scheme.

That historic design motifs do not always fit the needs of the problem is obviously apparent. It is to be admitted that enduring patterns of beauty have been accomplished at many periods, giving to the world some of its fine furniture, textiles, and architecture. Many of them had their primary value in their special settings. To uproot them and transplant them into an incongruous locale would be the height of bad taste, in simple violation of the principles of fitness and harmony. If Chippendale or William and Mary furniture is to be used in a modern setting, the entire room, if not the complete home, should be designed accordingly, if an appearance of incongruity is to be avoided. The intelligent designer should hence be given free rein to work with the total ensemble in mind from start to finish. Otherwise a conglomeration of unrelated elements is likely to result, as a room furnished with a Chinese rug, dainty French furniture in scarlet and gold, walls in modern paint tints, and wide rectangular windows with flower boxes, with Grecian urns and a Swiss clock on the mantel. There is no need for gross errors in design, nor is it necessary to spend lavishly to secure harmony in design. Even with very limited funds there can be an assembling of related and harmonious units if the plan is decided upon in advance. In any event the services of a designer can be sought for initial advice.

The same considerations apply to the painting of a picture. The young art student may study with profit the painting techniques of as many schools as his time and energies permit. He should, however, do this intelligently, taking into account the factors operating to influence the painter at each period: matters such as available pigments, mixing mediums, and materials, as well as prevailing subject matter and models. His own final technique need not be copied after any of those studied but could be a style he himself finds suited to his personality and interests, taking into account his own objectives as an artist, the kind of materials he will have available, the type of subject matter to feature, and other significant considerations.

Contemporary painters have freely borrowed—in fact, the borrowings, revampings, and restylizing has by no means been confined to commercial designers. Modern painters have, in some instances, experimented in attaining the manner employed by the painting of Persian miniatures, made use of Byzantine motifs, and followed suggestions from African sculpture, with varying success. To this end it is not necessary to leave one's native shores, for the museum affords abundant examples from which one may work. There are strong resemblances to Byzantine motifs in some of the work of Matisse; to African sculpture in some of Picasso's forms; to Central American jungle in the work of Rousseau. The crux of the process is the end result: does the product appear as a new and justifiable form effecting some new desirable art creation, or is it merely an exercise that results in a re-creation that is neither fish nor fowl? Usually the criterion of successful attainment will not be mere novelty or bizarre qualities but the attainment of more expressive character within the confines of fitness, unity, or related considerations. Grotesqueness, to be art, must be grotesqueness for a recognized purpose that furthers aesthetic and effective presentation of some definite quality, not merely for the trivial purpose of being different.

The creative and inventive minds are constantly alert for new ideas, new techniques, new forms, new results—but they are also aware that in a wealth of experimentation are a very limited number of really good creations that will satisfy the world as being definitely aesthetic creations. New ideas in art, as in all other areas of human endeavor, are relatively rare, but human gullibility is great.

BIBLIOGRAPHY

BENTON, T. *An Artist in America.* New York: McBride, 1937.

BEST-MAUGARD, A. *A Method for Creative Design.* New York: Knopf, 1927.

BINGHAM, W. *Aptitudes and Aptitude Testing.* New York: Harper, 1937.

BIRKHOFF, G. *Aesthetic Measure.* Cambridge: Harvard University Press, 1933.

CASSON, S. (ed.). *Artists at Work.* London: Harrap, 1933.

CHASE, JOSEPH C. *Creative Design.* New York: Wiley, 1934.

DODGE, A. *Occupational Ability Patterns.* New York: Teachers College, Columbia University, 1935.

DOWNEY, JUNE E. *Creative Imagination.* New York: Harcourt, 1929.

DREPS, H. F. "The Psychophysical Capacities and Abilities of College Art Students of High and Low Standing." *Psychol. Monogr.*, 1933, 45, 134–146.

FAURE, E. *History of Art.* Vol. V. *The Spirit of the Forms.* New York: Garden City Publishing Company, 1937.

FRANKL, PAUL T. *New Dimensions.* New York: Payson & Clarke, 1928.

FRANKL, PAUL T. *Form and Re-form.* New York: Harper, 1930.

FRY, R. E. *Vision and Design.* New York: Brentano's, 1938.

GALTON, F. *Hereditary Genius.* London: Macmillan, 1892.

HARTMAN, G. (ed.). *Creative Expression through Art.* Washington: Progressive Education Association, 1926.

HARTMAN, G., and ANN SCHUMAKER. *Creative Expression.* New York: Day, 1932.

HIRSCH, N. D. M. *Genius and Creative Intelligence.* Cambridge: Science-Art, 1931.

HOLLINGWORTH, L. *Gifted Children: Their Nature and Nurture.* New York: Macmillan, 1926.

HULL, C. *Aptitude Testing.* Yonkers: World Book, 1928.

JACOBS, M. *The Art of Composition.* New York: Doubleday, 1926.

KINTER, MADALINE. *The Measurement of Artistic Abilities.* New York: Psychological Corporation, 1933.

LULL, FERRIS, PARKER, *et al. The Evolution of Man*, Sigma Xi Lectures. New Haven: Yale University Press. 1922. IV, Angell, J. R. *The Evolution of Intelligence.*

McADORY, MARGARET. "The Construction and Validation of an Art Test." *Teach. Coll. Contr. Educ.*, 1933, No. 383.

McCLOY, W. "Creative Imagination in Children and Adults." *Psychol. Monogr.*, 1939, 51, 88–102.

MACRAE, A. *Talents and Temperament.* London: Nesbet, 1932.

MEIER, N. C. "Factors in Artistic Aptitude: Final Summary of a Ten-year Study of Special Ability." *Psychol. Monogr.*, 1939, 51, 140–158.

MEIER, N. C. "Reconstructive Imagination." *Psychol. Monogr.*, 1939, 51, 117–126.

MEIER, N. C. "Aesthetic Intelligence: Its Nature and Emergence." *Proc. Ninth Int. Cong. Psychol.*, 1929. Princeton: Psychol. Rev. Co., 1930, 305–306.

MEIER, N. C. *Aesthetic Judgment as a Measure of Art Talent.* Iowa City: State University of Iowa, 1926.

MEIER, N. C. *Can Art Talent Be Discovered by Test Devices?* Cincinnati: Western Art Association, 1927.

O'CONNOR, J. *Born That Way.* Baltimore: Williams & Wilkins, 1928.

REVESZ, G. *Formenwelt des Tastsinnes.* The Hague: Martinus Nyhoff, 1938. I. *Grundlegung der Haptik und der Blindenpschologie.* II. *Formasthetik und Plastik der Blinden.*

RIGNANO, E. *Upon the Inheritance of Acquired Characters.* Trans. by Basil Harvey. Chicago: Open Court, 1911.

ROSSMAN, J. *The Psychology of the Inventor.* Washington: Inventors Publishing Company, 1931.

SAUNDERS, A. W. "The Stability of Artistic Aptitude at the Child Level." *Psychol. Monogr.*, 1936, 48, 126–154.

SCHEINFELD, A. *You and Heredity.* New York: Stokes, 1939.

SPEARMAN, C. *The Abilities of Man, Their Nature and Measurement.* New York: Macmillan, 1927.

TEAD, O. *Instincts in Industry.* Boston: Houghton Mifflin, 1918, Chap. IV.

TERMAN, L., *et al. Genetic Studies of Genius.* Stanford University: Stanford University Press, 1925.

THOMSON, G. *The Factorial Analysis of Human Ability.* Boston: Houghton Mifflin, 1939.

THURSTONE, L. L. *Primary Mental Abilities.* Chicago: University of Chicago Press, 1938.

TIEBOUT, C. (MRS. R. MELAMPY). "The Psychophysical Functions Differentiating Artistically Superior from Artistically Inferior Children." *Psychol. Monogr.*, 1933, 45, 108–133.

TIEBOUT, C., and N. MEIER. "Artistic Ability and General Intelligence." *Psychol. Monogr.*, 1936, 48, 95–125.

VOSS, M. D. "Conditions Affecting the Functioning of the Art Appreciation Process at the Child-level." *Psychol. Monogr.*, 1936, 48, 1–39.

WRIGHT, W. H. *The Creative Will.* New York and London: Lane, 1916.

Chapter 5 · ART IN CONTEMPORARY HUMAN AFFAIRS

1. Psychological Factors in Modern Design

In Chap. 1 the viewpoint was advanced that art is ingrained in the human organism. It was never 'placed' there, nor did it appear only in man's later centuries; rather it gradually evolved through a common experience with consistencies in nature and in the life of man himself. In the process a limited number of relatively simple principles arose, as widely applicable criteria of value. In Chap. 2 the thesis was advanced that among a number of tenable theories of value in art, the most durable and generally satisfying one was that art is determined chiefly by two considerations, namely, attainment of qualities generally referred to as *principles*, and skillful or ingenious attainment of them in the work of art. In Chap. 3 it was shown that new and 'modern' art survives or perishes largely on the critical point of whether it is built upon sound aesthetic principles. The ways and means of attaining quality in art are inexhaustible: this fact is equally important whether the product is a typical art form—painting, architecture, sculpture, drama, the dance, or music—or any of the multitudinous applied aspects of art.

In any aspect, aesthetic appeal is normally found in a combination of skillful realization of aesthetic principles or qualities in a harmony or unity. But, of course, other factors enter into particular fields to become of greater or lesser importance.

In the field of *architecture* a close relationship exists between materials and design. The mud-block structure of the Taos Indians or the Saudi-Arabians is recognized as being far more fitting in its arid setting than a brick dwelling may be in Chicago. The steep-pitched Norwegian dwelling not only reduces snow load but aesthetically harmonizes with the gross forms of the spruce tree. Similarly, the Chinese pagoda and the Japanese temple resemble the downward-branching evergreen trees (particularly some varieties of pine and spruce). The Japanese temple roof is likewise designed along functional considerations inasmuch as the frequent rains necessitate a design affording wide coverage without the necessity of steep pitch. The relation of materials, function, and design is likewise present in the massive forms of Egyptian edifices, where native stone is abundant, thick walls provide cool interiors, and massive columns support the heavy construction. In these instances the design is likely to be pleasing since construction through choice of fitting material (or accidental selection) more or less automatically leads to adoption of harmonious design.

Yet, in America, despite these simple considerations, a major portion of New World architecture has been dictated by tradition, leading to monstrosities and indefensible creations. Bank buildings have been designed as Greek temples, libraries as Gothic cathedrals, stadia from Roman aqueduct motifs, prairie residences as French chateaus, city dwellings as Cotswold farmhouses, and public buildings as mausoleums. Instances of the building having a functional design are noteworthy,[1] but they are a small minority. Change seems to take place very slowly, with earlier details retained long after their

---

[1] Fisk University Library; Empire State Building; Gruntvig Church, Copenhagen; Bely Shop, Paris; Tribune Building (Saarinen design), Chicago.

functional utility has passed—even after their decorative need is no longer apparent.

'Modern' edifices do not necessarily represent an advance: they do only in the event simplicity and functional design are

 conducive to greater congruity, harmony, and allover unity—in short if they disclose a more effective attainment of aesthetic quality through good use of principles along with functional utility.

Climate has been a factor affecting design in considerable measure. It is commonplace that the Gothic cathedral is a design serving needs in a region where there are dull, rainy days as well as bright, sunny ones, the tall narrow window openings providing illumination for both. But in the normally sunny and warm Mediterranean countries, the Italian design provided for cool interiors and a reduction of the brilliant light; likewise the mosque took into account the need for cool, spacious interiors and a

Fig. 36. Saarinen design for Tribune tower. Functional design exemplifying structural unity. *Courtesy of Fogg Museum, Harvard University.*

minimum of light. To the far north, Swedish church architecture concentrated upon heavy masonry and narrow, slitlike openings, as a proper protection from the cold winters. On the Japanese islands, with a climate lacking continental extremes of temperature, thin walls and flimsy bamboo construction are plentifully employed. In each region the design may be fitting and the materials conducive for realization of principles.

Interiors likewise have tended to adhere to traditional forms. The American dwelling of the nineties provided for the needs of large families. Its setting was a spacious lawn. When apartments grew in popularity along with increasing urbanization and families of decreasing size, design lagged far behind the trend. The so-called efficiency apartment was an experiment stimulated by failure of apartment design to supply modern urban needs. Its introduction required furniture designers to give attention to space-conserving ideas. The artist, now serving as interior decorator, was called upon to suggest colors and lines that carried the illusion of added space when redesign alone had reached an apparent limit. In the process there was considerable attainment of simplicity and harmony that earlier traditional design lacked. The functional utility of every piece previously regarded as needed was questioned. The impetus was caught up by the paint manufacturers, and new products accelerated the changes toward more aesthetically satisfying living quarters, held in check only by prejudice for the old themes, with economic conditions limiting the extent of replacement or new construction.

Costume design has had a somewhat similar history. Human proportions have changed little in the course of history, but costume has run through cycles of changes. Modern dress is by no means the most beautiful.[1] Research has shown that even present-day women rate costumes of the sixteenth and seventeenth centuries superior to current or recent dress design. When girls and women of even isolated regions have been shown drawings depicting typical costumes over the past five centuries, judgments expressed and derived through the paired-comparisons procedure have favored costumes of

---

[1] JACOBSON, WILHELMINA. "Basic Aesthetic Factors in Costume Design." *Psychol. Monogr.*, 1933, 45, 147–184.

various periods, even though the subjects were unfamiliar
with the times in which they were worn. This result tends
to discredit the view often met that dress tends to follow familiarity and is biased toward those creations serving utility of
the moment. Some of the hoop-skirt modes were admired
greatly, yet none of the women expressing judgments had
ever worn one or ever seen one on a living person.

The basis for preference must hence lie in a wholly different
direction than suitability for the person reacting to the design
or than conformity to conventional standards or current style.
It must be also independent of individual or personal interest
and application, expressed in the view of "how it would look
on me." By experimental and case-study methods, Dr.
Jacobson derived the conclusion that judgments such as those
expressed by her subjects rest chiefly on the criterion of aesthetic principles of rhythm, sequence, and balance.

Functional utility has, however, intervened to disqualify
most of these earlier designs for present use. The wearer could
not enter modern motorcars, elevators, or cafés; or, if that
feat were accomplished, few others would then be able to
enjoy the limited space remaining. In view of this difficulty,
no attempt is made to revive the costumes, greater beauty
being sought in quite another direction—having the costume
so designed as to feature a natural embodiment of beauty—
the human form. Hence the salvation of contemporary
costume design lies in two directions—preserving the inherent
beauty in the human form and permitting as much decoration
as can be effected through control of lines and accents, with,
of course, harmonious color. The problem resolves itself into
one of building aesthetic design onto a form already basic to
the process. In the combination may ensue expression of
rhythm, balance, transition, harmony, and other qualities
limited only by the aesthetic sensitivity and resourcefulness
of the designer.

The *automobile* and the *airplane* have a history not unlike other developments, with the difference that they have been evolved in the short space of a few decades. It is striking, nonetheless, to witness the difficulty with which the automobile finally extricated itself from the carriage design, and the airplane from the box-kite or bird-with-wings analogy. In both the influence of materials is marked. Without means of suitably fashioning sheet steel for the automobile body and duralumin for the airplane neither would have attained its present development as quickly. Certainly in these two machines there is the perfect exemplification of the process of adapting materials to design and design to function where the result is an embodiment of beauty. The search for the ideal of streamlining was essentially a quest for simplification, unity, rhythm, and other aesthetic qualities. The effort of one manufacturer to borrow from the Roman arch, the fleur-de-lis, and other traditional design patterns served only temporarily because these were merely *units* in the design, not necessarily related to the unity of the entire form. It was soon found that the design should begin with a complete conception of the *outward* appearance of the whole design as a single unit.[1] In many of the design laboratories considerable numbers of possible designs are made in clay, papier-mâché, or wood, leaving detailed development until after the basic design of the unit has been decided.

Innovation in Commercial Uses of Art. Just as in the case of the automobile, which attracts no longer by its mechanical features but rather by beauty of design, so also the marketing of modern wares must be done with consideration for artistic qualities. The product must not only be good to look upon,

---

[1] This end is still not attained by some models that appear as a body merely attached to wheels that are not *aesthetically* proportioned to the design and size of the body. Tire shape and size need to be taken into account with *each* change in body design.

but it must be presented to a critical public in a pleasing and forceful way. Particularly is this vital to the product that involves considerable contemplation before purchase. The design of radio cabinets, as an instance of a new article not yet quite stabilized, has passed through a succession of stages, including excessive embellishment to severe plainness, and through a complete gamut of color and material finishes, both natural and simulated. Here again, the dictates of selection must, to be really satisfying, take into account both the design and finish of the cabinet and the surroundings where it is to be placed. The cabinet itself should be a unity, and its placement should not violate the conditions required for harmony and fitness with its setting.

Modern advertising art has utilized artistic talent available in the metropolitan centers and much talent of the ingenious type. Since advertising has as its first function the getting and holding of attention, the artist has at times employed a number of compositional devices: distortion of form, color, and size, unusual perspective, position distortion, creation of an illusion of infinite space, and use of humor through unusual treatment. In the better layouts aesthetic qualities are in evidence—balance, sequence of forms and color, and unity. Frequently the layout exemplifies a number of qualities so well contrived and attained as to elicit the highest admiration. The layout man and collaborating artists are driven by competitive necessity to produce the best of which they are capable.[1]

2. ART IN SOCIAL CONTROL

The control of attitudes widely held by the public has been shared by the spoken voice, the printed page, and pictorial

---

[1] In a recent study by Joseph Kochwasser using selected layouts both spectacular and aesthetic with others having both qualities, it was found that the former had the greater attention value, but the aesthetic type proved to be more effective for recall. University of Iowa master's thesis.

creations. Although the latter have not always deserved
classification as art, many of the products have been meritorious both as good compositions and as effective stimuli in

FIG. 37. "Must be that Kansas Spinach." The effectiveness of this cartoon
lies in the prior establishment of the character 'Popeye' as the popular
symbol of audacious, confident might. The strips provide a basis for the
cartoon. *Courtesy of J. N. (Ding) Darling and the Des Moines Register—New
York Herald Tribune.*

influencing the public mind. Sometimes the printed appeal
has been supplemented by the picture, and at other times the
two have worked side by side. Even the comic strip today

exerts a significant effect upon public thinking as well as affording genuine entertainment. Social and economic theories have been presented through subtle suggestion in the comic strip. Reflections upon both serious and trivial aspects of living have found their way into the pleasantries and banalities of some of the strips. They furthermore establish conventional imagery or stereotypes useful in social communication and as ready-made bases for characterizing other objects and individuals. In a few instances admirable draftsmanship and color work have been lavished on the humorous characters and the settings in which they appear.[1]

Some of these strips are important through the very fact that millions of people read them daily. They are important additionally because they frequently employ a subtle flattery of the reader. The creator of one widely read strip explained to the author that his strip has its appeal through two characteristics—'*hokum*' and *continuity*. No reader actually believes that his child character could do all the miraculous and unbelievably clever stunts this creator has her doing, yet the suspense from day to day induced by the continuity leads many readers to turn to the particular strip as a first interest in taking up the paper; and it is in this strip that suggestions regarding capital and labor relationships, individualism, and other social philosophies have been presented. Psychologically, some of the strips afford the reader an emotional letdown or a considerable amount of wish fulfillment. The reader sees in the juvenile character just those things that he would like to have done when he was a child, or he sees in a 'roughneck' character the debunking of many of the shams and inconsistencies of modern life. It is just the sort of exposé the reader would like to undertake. At various times the creator of a comic strip has taken his characters through political cam-

---

[1] Bringing Up Father, Terry and the Pirates, *et al.*

paigns, through court trials, through heart-rending human interest episodes in the course of which reflections upon the injustices or the deficiencies of social institutions have been clearly demonstrated. In the hands of the true artist and

FIG. 38. "Looking over the Possibilities for the Next Fight." Depends for its coverage upon the public's familiarity with the analogy of the bull in the china shop. *Courtesy of J. N. Darling and the Des Moines Register—New York Herald Tribune.*

student of society, both the comic strip and the political cartoon offer unlimited openings for satiric comment on all phases of life—political, religious, economic, and sociological.

3. The Social Psychology of Attitude Control

The effective caricaturists[1] achieve their greatness by possessing a wide knowledge of public affairs and familiarity with personalities in public life. In addition the able caricaturist knows the public he serves. He is aware of the typical education, both formal and informal, that most of his public have experienced. He is familiar with the Bible, Mother Goose legends, Aesop's *Fables*. The characteristic traits of members of the animal kingdom, of birds and other forms of life are to him more than ordinarily familiar. He is skilled in the delineation of these forms; he has the ability to transmute a likeness of a public figure into that of any of the forms in order to transfer to the person a trait possessed by the animal. On occasion, he can merge the unmistakable likeness of a well-known personality into that of a fish or a fussy old hen or a braying donkey. Into the characteristic likeness of a prominent figure may be imputed on occasion the unmistakable attributes of greed, overbearingness, humility, or the stereotype of the conventional business or professional man.

The process of social control through caricature commonly takes two forms: the *evoking of social displeasure* or the *building up of social acceptance*. In the height of a campaign the former procedure may take any one of the following directions: the object of the caricaturist's attention may carry the suggestion of identity with a previously established questionable character; it may carry the suggestion of undesirable features or possibly a trait such as duplicity or reprehensible indifference to realities. The features may be distorted to the extent of making the person objectionable to many readers by suggesting weakness of character or by invoking an unethical attitude or despicable trait.

---

[1] Thomas Nast, J. T. McCutcheon, Jay N. Darling, Rollin Kirby—to mention a few.

On the other hand, social *acceptance* may be steadily built
by identifying the person consistently with admired stereotypes of the masses. The individual may be shown in boyhood

FIG. 39. "Having Such a Good Time." Presumed Democratic celebration
following the 1936 election is here depicted by Darling in a masterful
handling of the donkey form—as mortician, carpenter, minister, singers,
etc., with ingenious organization. *Courtesy of J. N. Darling and the Des Moines
Register—New York Herald Tribune.*

days as a carefree, typical American lad plunging into the
old swimming hole or trudging along the road with a willow-
branch fishing pole over his shoulder. He may be made to

appear as a rugged Mickey McGuire type, ready for anything. His opponent may be pictured as a boy growing up in the lap of luxury with a pompous butler escorting him across a spacious lawn with the child dressed in lace and shiny shoes.

Fig. 40. Moon Mullins. By 1928 this humorous character had become the nation's stereotype for good-natured irresponsibility. *Courtesy of Frank Willard and Chicago Tribune–New York Daily News Syndicate.*

The features of a colorless and ordinary individual may be 'revised' to provide him with a firm square-set jaw, a determined judicial look, clear, commanding eye, and glasses to carry the suggestion of the businessman who really gives attention to the fine points of operating his business. One noted cartoonist explained to the author that he worked the better part of a month before he got the physiognomy he had been seeking, which was one that, in the author's judgment, contributed heavily to the 1924 success of Calvin Coolidge.

A subtle type of pictorial-verbal device for controlling opinion is the graphic editorial, which carries to the front page selected pithy items from the paper's program or statements just enunciated by a public figure. The cartoon space is usually divided vertically into two or three boxes, each one

containing some drawn pose or action of the public figure and
the other some cogent section of a speech or special quotation.
The effect of the practice is twofold. More readers have their

Fig. 41. Compare the striding figure with the striding form of Moon Mullins
in Fig. 40. The resemblance, even though accidental, permits a transfer of
qualities associated with the comic-strip character, a circumstance for which
prior conditioning prepared the reader. *Courtesy of J. T. McCutcheon and the
Chicago Tribune.*

attention directed to the pithy portions of the speech (which
would not be read at all by many readers), and the reading is
done with the idealized figure in the field of attention. The

individual gains in public estimation in a twofold manner: the idealized appearance is experienced coincidental with his best utterance.

4. ART AND ATTITUDES TOWARD SOCIAL INSTITUTIONS AND STATE POLICY

War as a social institution, however decried and condemned, is still with us. The outbreak of war in 1939 would seem to indicate a failure of all forms of propagandist control, including art, for war has had its full store of attention. Literature has contributed its score of best sellers; the cinema and the stage have dramatized them; painting and sculpture have put in their bit. The cartoon has outdone itself in exposing the inconsistencies and shaky logic of disarmament conferences, nationalistic aspirations, and the aggressor nation in actual war. Figure 42 is much in point. The cartoonist draws his effectiveness (potential if not evident in results) from his power to take simple analogies and drive them home.

The Japanese invasion of China, the First World War, and conflict at other times has brought forth many clever and studied efforts on the part of caricaturists to satirize points of view. In some instances these efforts have been directed toward promoting the avowed policy of a given newspaper, in other instances they have represented a combination of the newspaper's social philosophy and that of the individual cartoonist, and in still other instances they have represented merely the individual cartoon's satirical comment on the war institution itself. These efforts may be reflections of the nation's current attitude, they may be the reflections of majority groups, or they may be the bold attempt to register a protest against what may be regarded as an institution of definitely sinister character.

During periods of national crises such as times when the nation is actually at war, the cartoonist may become an agent for the intentional promotion of attitudes calculated to arouse and intensify attitudes already known to be existent. He

FIG. 42. One aspect of the war problem. Graphic satire; pithy criticism with a touch of ironic humor. *Courtesy of J. N. Darling and the Des Moines Register— New York Herald Tribune.*

therefore may become an extremely effective propagandist. Not only because of the usual effectiveness that pictorial material normally enjoys but because of the increased tempo of excitement, people have less time and patience with lengthy

FIG. 43. Subtle comment upon current policy and attitudes, utilizing the satire at the same time to constitute a subtle thrust at trends in the field of art. *Courtesy of J. N. Darling and the Des Moines Register—New York Herald Tribune.*

discussions and therefore give more time to the quickly comprehended cartoon.

The propaganda value of the cartoon as an instrument promoting pacifism or militarism is subject to certain conditions that were the subject of recent research by Albert D. Annis. Dr. Annis found by carefully controlled procedures that, where the policy of the paper presumably requires the cartoonist to strike at the institution repeatedly, the propaganda effect of the cartoon is greatly enhanced, as contrasted with the type of cartoon that merely comments. In this study it was found that an occasional cartoon, however well drawn and however aesthetic it may be in design, may be less effective than a cartoon, less well drawn and even poorly designed, that carries a definite arousal of related attitudes already known to be adverse to the institution.

5. Art in Political Psychology

Mussolini, Hitler, and Stalin have made art an instrument in rendering their respective programs effective. Lenin, before Stalin, recognized that a partly illiterate nation could not be maneuvered easily by verbal symbols. Graphic symbols, graphic suggestions, and graphic slogans and concepts had to be invoked. Hence the wide use of the hammer and sickle, the ubiquitous portraits of a glorified Lenin (now Stalin) in some instances thirty feet high, and the posting of billboards depicting propaganda of the system: decrepit Capitalism and youthful, healthy Communism.

Hitler organized some of the world's greatest and most impressive spectacles of might. A crowd of 100,000 was not uncommon; whether mustered or 'advised' matters little. The setting was worthy of good stage designers, utilizing color and lighting with strong effect. Both Hitler and Mussolini used the technique of psychological conditioning much as does the cartoonist: striving for the idealized or glorified *Hitler the Leader*, or *Mussolini the Duce*, selecting only those views that show most tellingly the strong profile or set jaw. Hitler has

caused to be set forth the ideal German manhood and woman-
hood type, much as the Greeks did or as we might point to the
Apollo or Venus.

In such a program of national unity, suggestions were available from the church, which has long used symbols and seeks
a simplified, centered interest. In fact the national fanaticism
of a revived political state may be equally as devoted and as
intense as a religious revival and quite as emotionally moving.
And it is easily possible that the relatively less effective
democracy is less efficient (allegedly) by its very decentraliza-
tion and lack of tangible symbol and definite program: the
fanatic's devoted urge to serve the state is lacking. In the
democracy there are *many* actual or potential leaders; consequently, no well-established, single symbol of aggressive,
single-minded might, no heroic countenance confronting the
citizen at every turn.[1]

In 1940–1941 the two surviving large democracies tardily
effected some steps toward national unity. Great Britain
succeeded in utilizing the Churchill personality as the symbol
of indomitable courage and of British tenacity. His square-
jawed countenance epitomized the resolution of an entire
people for determined resistance to anything the axis powers
might launch. From these innumerable photographs the
caricaturist was afforded material for deepening the expression and in many other ways reinforcing the unifying process.

The United States found its task less ready-made. Although
President Roosevelt, by speech and act, maintained a defiant
attitude, it remained for a variety of activities and personalities to cultivate by gradual stages the morale desired for
national effectiveness in the critical times. These took the

---

[1] An exception occurred during the monetary crisis of 1933, when the widely
distributed portrait of President Roosevelt, expressing calm, reassuring confidence, provided a definite factor in restoring public equanimity and spirit of
restored hope.

usual forms and some unusual ones. Music served by reviving "God Bless America," and the appeal was extended through small banners and placards. The poster did its usual stint. Pageants and drama carried out the theme of totalitarian brutality and duplicity. Literature contributed mightily (*Out of the Night, The Voice of Destruction,* etc.). Churchill's speeches were offered as the book of the hour, and predictions were made that the art qualities of some of his utterances would place them among the great literature of all time.

Among the unusual forms of morale building the comic strip shifted to the war (defense) setting, almost overnight in some instances, gradually in others. In Little Orphan Annie, Daddy Warbucks returned from an unnamed concentration camp and in almost no time at all had great mills turning out war (defense) materials. Assisting him in combating sabotage, were his two aids Asp and Punjab. In Winnie Winkle the Hollywood venture was suddenly terminated by Will's joining up with a detachment comprised of old college friends. Jane Arden was soon on the trail of *saboteurs* and foreign agents. Years previously the excellent strip Terry and the Pirates (excellent particularly in draftsmanship) had been interesting the American public in the Far East situation; now it was a relatively simple matter to introduce the sinister Kiel and move operations toward the commerce raider, and from the "invader" to operators of obvious nationality.

It is not likely that such aspects of applied art exert an important influence upon national morale; but the effects are probably more far-reaching than is usually estimated. The reader in the Army camp or in the Navy training center is impressed with the evidence shown of general interest in the program of which he is a part. The strip sequence (such as Winnie Winkle) tends to make military service the only honorable thing to do when opportunity comes. The Orphan Annie sequence suggests to the capitalist that unstinted devotion and sacrifice is the expected thing of him. Since the specific individuals to whom the idea is addressed *and* the supporting public at large are both imbued with the same idea, social pressure is in the making to facilitate the complete system of attitudes. This may be democracy's way of inducing supporting attitudes in place of the *enforced* directed attitudes in the totalitarian state. Its effectiveness is perhaps limited, since most individuals need more than suggestion to alter habits and attitudes of long standing. The engendered public opinion, however, may make the transition more certain for the individual who is at all susceptible to the opinion of society and of his associates, even if it does not readily awaken in him some sense of responsibility or awareness of a greater self-interest to be served by compliance with the general will.

In periods of crisis, it becomes even more essential that any graphic appeal be designed to utilize the preformed concepts and other aspects of experience common to most of the population. In the design of a poster, aesthetic qualities alone are not enough; the theme and presentation of the appeal should capitalize upon *favorable* past experience or established attitudes of the observer. If there is associated with the earlier experience a strong emotional context, this will be transferred to the poster, giving to the object of the poster's appeal the immediate benefit of strongly reinforced emotional support. The process is perfectly realized in the poster illustrated (Fig. 44). Most English-speaking persons are familiar with Kipling's immortal *Lest we forget, lest we forget*. The artist has merely turned one word of the phrase to a similar term which not only picks up the Kipling phrase with all its solemnity and foreboding but adds by the substitution a more dire consequence, all too graphically suggested in the barren setting of the poster's ground. A more thought-inducing appeal could hardly have been conceived, if one grants the validity of the logic involved in the particular cause it represents.

Structurally, aesthetically, and psychologically the poster represents design at its best; hence it occasions no surprise that the jury and public agreed in judging it the best.

Fig. 44. Poster by Arthur Hawkins. See text. *Courtesy of Committee to Defend America by Aiding the Allies.*

By 1940 it had become clear that two factors, at least, accounted for Greater Germany's sequence of successes: first, superior military power made possible by intensive preparation by a people trained in versatile industrial production. The Rhine Valley and north central Europe has been since the Middle Ages the major workshop of Europe. Economic and natural selection has operated to make of these peoples the artisans capable of turning out, when guided or commandeered to do so, machines of destruction, as well as watches, cameras, typewriters, and precision instruments in time of peace. Second, the factor of fanatic national unity, skillfully welded by propagation of beliefs in past injustices needing rectification, and belief in a great destiny. This appeal took various forms, including even the great incentive of bringing better economic and political organization to peoples they must first bring into the orbit of their control.

It was to these ends that Hitler and his co-workers designed the colossal spectacles, focusing attention upon his oratorical appeals for unity in carrying out the objectives. Not only was the arresting fanfare of trumpets and other musical introductions employed, but the rostrum was backed by gigantic magenta silk banners, forming part of an impressive design. On occasions tens of thousands of people were assembled and maintained ordered participation as occasion dictated—by respectful attention, vociferous applause, or the chanting of a party slogan. By means of radio the address and the thunderous earmarks of unity were carried to all parts of the Reich. The art of the occasion was not confined to the spectacle itself, but included psychological suggestion carried in the resolute, firm, confident tone and voice of the leader. In a situation such as this no oratory need be more than that to have maximal effectiveness.

It is often observed that a monarchy, socialistic despotism, fascist despotism, or any form of totalitarianism in which control of the major portion of the nationalistic thinking of the people is under rigid state control, is more powerful through its centralized control than any government permitting unlimited expression of opinion of its people and free access of any person or group to the instruments of propaganda. When the caricaturist may at will criticize the chief executive or the chief of staff of the Army or the chief justice of the supreme court with utter impunity, when the satiric writer may expose inconsistencies and irrationality in the conduct of foreign relations, and when the dramatist may produce plays exposing the shams and shortcomings in the administration of government bureaus, the net effect is a tendency to weaken faith in the efficiency of the form of government. Furthermore, it is argued, such diverse cross-currents of thought can only neutralize—seldom reinforce—national unity.

In the totalitarian state there is singleness of purpose, created and furthered by one directing impulse—state-induced thinking by one continuous propaganda campaign: that of the state. Nonconforming artists, writers, dramatists, and political thinkers are silenced. In the other system, approximated by the free democracy, any propagandistic enterprise may flourish and may attempt in any manner to further its particular view or program.

Yet, as the world moves into recurrent tests toward the eventual stability of the two opposed ideologies, the role of art seems destined to play a somewhat obscured but exceedingly important part. Supreme tests requiring the ultimate endurance of whole nations may devolve upon a single crucial factor: morale. And in this final measure of the struggle the outcome may be decided by the relative degree of resoluteness behind the individual citizen's effort. Bedrock conviction of the worth of the ideal for which he is to make unlimited sacrifice may in the last analysis decide the eventual outcome.

Viewed in a specific way it becomes a question of how the individual arrives at his conviction. If he is compelled to accept as imposed from above one line of thought, however plausible and appealing, without the privilege of examining and evaluating in the light of full knowledge, he may, by chance discovery of conflicting ideas or through counter propaganda from without, have his original conviction impaired. If doubt takes root, disintegration may be rapid.

If, on the other hand, the free and unlimited presentation of many relative considerations including vital ones is permitted to come to the attention of the free citizen, he will then, of his own volition, adopt a firm and unshakable conviction of the rightness of his position. If the democracy's cause is just and fair, viewed in a long-time perspective, and opportunity has been afforded for a full envisagement of the problem in all its important aspects, the full power of the democracy, while slowly engendered, may become of formidable proportions.

In this process the role of the unregimented artist may be all important. Replacing the fiat of the leader or clique then in power, he senses and interprets the thought-out will of the whole people. Being of the people, he works on and with the people. Great forces are envisaged and translated into understandable form for the citizen's examination and reaction. Not all his efforts will be responded to positively. The public will reject some flatly. But since it is the final judge, the resultant selection will ordinarily reflect considerable common-sense wisdom. In the process the caricaturist may see through attractive but misleading pretensions; through half truths and sham social nostrums, and hold them up to scorn through the device of satire. Complex ideological systems may be reduced to simple terms and characterized in analogies that everyone can understand.

On the side of positive contribution, the artist, the dramatist, the satiric writer can by constructive analysis further a deepened understanding of the form of government he favors. If it has greater virtues than faults he can transmute some objective aspects of the virtue into easily comprehensible realities. In time of crisis he can make indefinite dangers appear dramatic and near at hand and turn vague misgivings into concrete dread. Poster art played an important role in the war of 1914–1918 in all countries, and in the United States materially stimulated individual participation in loan, enlistment, food, and shipbuilding drives. Met with at every turn, it served to catch, hold, and sustain attention to the job in hand and to reinforce determination.

FIG. 45. Perhaps no better or more succinct presentation of totalitarianism could be made. *Courtesy of J. T. McCutcheon and the Chicago Tribune.*

As serviceable as these functions of art in national destiny are, they will probably never be maximal, in the day-by-day influence upon the thinking of the people, until art attracts to its ranks the best from among all those available. Present-day society rewards most handsomely those who carry on the production-consumption process. It does not promise much to the youth who insists upon an art career. Even education, which is itself relatively underpaid, strives to follow, not revise, the conventional ascendance of business and industry, relegating art to the nonessential category in the minimum educational program. Art has received consistent and ungrudging support mainly in those localities that are contiguous to industry, which has learned that a public will prefer to buy products of good design.

Training the art student for envisagement of social and political problems and dynamic, aggressive, and clever ways of transmuting critical comment and analysis of these problems into cartoons, paintings, and drama of powerful appeal is still but dimly conceived and timidly approached. There are those who decry such proposals. But it cannot be ignored that much of the world's great art was conceived with deep feeling and was designed to glorify and advance religious, political, or social personages and ideals. Cultural anthropology reveals the intimate and necessary functions rendered by the artisan and artist as a co-worker with the priest class in social control of the group. Why, then, should the artist be of any lesser importance today? Why should he not be even more intimately concerned with human destiny, clarifying to the people the best thinking of the enlightened leader?

There is no reason why the artist type may not someday also be trained in economics, political science, psychology, and sociology and, with this preparation matured through travel and contact with industry, agriculture, commerce, and finance, then fill himself with public and international affairs and draw a cartoon only when he believes he has some idea of real worth to present. In other words, the *research cartoonist or the editorializing artist deserves a high place in current affairs.* Only by enjoying complete freedom can their best be produced. And their contributions are somewhat conditioned by their background facilities for understanding and interpreting the world as they know it. In an era of complex forces and intricate social organization such persons would be destined to play an important role.

6. INTERRELATION OF APPLIED AND FINE ART

The appearance of art in political pageantry, religious symbolism, commercial marketing aids, and the manifold aspects of social control inevitably tends to confuse the individual in his understanding of the nature of art itself. Even the expert struggles with this dilemma and at times declares that any use of graphic expression having for its purpose propaganda or social control of any kind cannot be true art. Likewise, the professional artist frequently disdains his practical-minded gentry who use graphic expression for business and commercial purposes.

Although there is undoubtedly some basis for observations such as those mentioned, it must be pointed out that in the larger world-and-time perspective these discriminations are more artificial than real. Art did not originate and develop in the studio; at no time was even Greek sculpture divorced from the life of the times, nor is it possible to find any real separation during the Renaissance of subject matter and motives from the prevailing religious philosophy. Some of the finest works of all time have been made possible through the patronage and support of personal or institutional interests.

Examining the interrelations even more deeply, it would be found that all phases of culture, and art is no exception, have been produced by a close interaction of practical incentives with more leisurely and studied independent development. The one offers suggestions for the other—each contributes to the other's progress. Though art creation is perhaps independently pursued more than other activities, it has essentially and inevitably a social character exhibiting all the phenomena of community of ideas and disclosing aspects of the phenomena of fashion imitation. It has its creative geniuses and its imitators. Sometimes the imitators may veer away from the original to the extent that a new and better idiom is begun or a superior product achieved. All this is inevitably true in a social world where individual differences are probably more imagined than exist in actuality.

If the position is taken that art is something greater than the products now assembled in museums, that art is intimately related and always has been with the affairs of mankind, that art through uses that to some appear perverse or misguided is functionally serviceable to mankind: if these viewpoints are envisaged in their true world-and-time perspective, then we may look upon art as a vital and important force in world affairs and upon the artist as a useful and significant man among men.

BIBLIOGRAPHY

BEHRENDT, W. C. *Modern Building: Its Nature, Problems and Forms.* New York: Harcourt, 1937.

BINDER, J. *Color in Advertising.* London: Studio, 1934.

BROWNELL, B., and F. L. WRIGHT. *Architecture and Modern Life.* New York: Harper, 1938.

BURRIS-MEYER, E. *Color and Design in the Decorative Arts.* New York: Prentice-Hall, 1935.

CAHILL, H. (ed.). *New Horizons in American Art.* New York: Museum of Modern Art, 1936.

CHARLOT, J. *Art from the Mayan to Disney.* New York: Sheed & Ward, 1939.

CIRCLE (J. L. Martin, Ben Nicholson, and N. Gabo, eds.). *International Survey of Constructive Art.* London: Faber, 1937.

CLOSS, H. *Art and Life.* New York: Stokes, 1936.

COLLINS, M., and O. RILEY. *Art Appreciation.* New York: Harcourt, 1933.

DOBSON, M. *Art Appreciation.* London: Putnam, 1932.

ELLIOTT, HUGER. *Fashions in Art.* New York: Appleton, 1937.

FAULKNER, RAY. *Art Today*. Minneapolis: University of Minnesota Press, 1936.

FRANKL, PAUL T. *New Dimensions*. New York: Payson & Clarke, 1928.

FRANKL, PAUL T. *Form and Re-form*. New York: Harper, 1930.

FRIEND, LEON, and JOSEPH HEFTER. *Graphic Design*. New York: McGraw-Hill, 1936.

GILL, ERIC. *Art in a Changing Civilization*. London: Lane, 1934.

GOLDSTEIN, H., and V. GOLDSTEIN. *Art in Every Day Life*. New York: Macmillan, 1932, rev. ed.

GROPIUS, W. *The New Architecture and the Bauhaus*. London: Faber, 1935.

HAGGERTY, M. *Art a Way of Life*. Minneapolis: University of Minnesota Press, 1935.

HITCHCOCK, H. R., and P. JOHNSON. *The International Style: Architecture since 1922*. New York: Norton, 1932.

HITCHCOCK, H. *Modern Architecture*. New York: Payson & Clark, 1929.

HOLME, G. *Industrial Design and the Future*. London: Studio, 1934.

HOLME, G. (ed.). *Art in the U.S.S.R.* London: Studio, 1936.

JACOBSON, WILHELMINA E. "An Experimental Investigation of the Basic Aesthetic Factors in Costume Design." *Psychol. Monogr.*, 1933, 45, 147–184.

KATZ, D. *The World of Colour*. London: Routledge, 1935.

KORN, A. *Glas im Bau und als Gebrachsgegenstand*. Berlin-Charlottenburg: Ernest Pollak Verlag, 1929.

LECORBUSIER [JEANNERET-GRIS, C. E.]. 1934–1938. Zurich: Girsbugee, 1939.

LONDON, KURT. *The Seven Soviet Arts*. New Haven: Yale University Press, 1938.

LUCKIESH, M. *Color and Its Applications*. New York: Van Nostrand, 1931.

NEWTON, E. *The Architect and the Public*. London: Allen & Unwin, 1935.

PARK, E. *New Backgrounds for a New Age*. New York: Harcourt, 1927.

SCHMECKEBIER, L. *Modern Mexican Art*. Minneapolis: University of Minnesota Press, 1939.

STURGES, R. *Interdependence of the Arts of Design*. Chicago: McClurg, 1905.

Appendix · CREATIVE ARTISTS AT WORK

Some creative artists of high rank possess definite ideas in regard to the process through which the products of their labor come into being. It is hence enlightening to present their own observations and ideas of creative artistic activity as they have personally experienced them. The content of this section is based upon notes of the author set down immediately following extensive contacts with the artists. These were prearranged meetings in connection with the Carnegie study of artistic capacity, some of them being made while the author was living temporarily in the communities (artists' colonies) and others during incidental or special trips. The contacts, varying from a period of several hours to repeated visits or an entire day, afforded ample opportunity to get an adequate expression from each artist of his ideas of artistic capacity, what he believed to be the hereditary basis or the part environment played, what he considered to be the traits of capacity, the role of intelligence, emotion, and other factors in artistic creation. His particular and individual manner of work was in some cases presented with considerable adequacy. Because of its detailed nature, notes are in some instances summarized and material not regarded as of particular significance omitted or reproduced only in part.

I

B,[1] believes that artistic capacity is not hereditary except through finely organized constitution: *i.e.*, good eyes, fine percep-

---

[1] The name, date, and complete notebook data are in the author's possession. It was deemed advisable here to use only the initial of the artist because of the following reasons: all artists change their techniques, manner of work, and

tion, sensitive emotionality, and good intelligence. He believes there is no separation of emotion and intelligence and that both are required for the best effects. His father was a noted orchestra leader; wife, a craftsman artist in her own right; one daughter disclosed interest in drawing and painting from the second year on. He believes artists should be more than mere colorists—they should know composition (*B* used the word "design"). Schools can give him technique: he must learn the design end by long, hard work. An artist may sometimes be lazy and play with color; he may occasionally overcolor, trying for interesting effects, but he will stagnate at that level if he does not supplement his emotional interest in color effects by serious study of design. *B* holds that the artist should always begin with a definite motive determined by the emotional effect (somber, sunlit, earthy, peculiar or uncommon lighting, etc.) and adhere to that throughout his painting. No rules, formulas, or maxims are of avail. He must feel his way until he has the effect he desires, which in some instances may require months or a year of high-pressure worry and concern. The better artist is never satisfied but has to stop sometime.

It is very important that a painter should be able to criticize his own work. He is hopeless if he is easily satisfied or if he adheres to one system. Hence a slavish adherence to the idea of *Impressionism* will lead him to sterile production. He should be alert to the values and procedures of others. All peoples and races, *B* believes from his observations, have about the same proportion of talented individuals, whether they be artists, musicians, or writers. The Southwest Indians, including the children, do surprising things, particularly attractive by virtue of their *simplicity* and *sincerity*.

An artist must first be motivated by the feeling that the subject he is contemplating is worth painting. It is a futile waste of time to attempt ordinary scenes or settings. It is hence very important that

---

interests from time to time. The account given herein is true only for the period when the contact was made. It will hence be more desirable to assume that the statement represents a particular artist at a particular time and that, while it is very probable that the description fits other artists as well, simple prudence would dictate that the artists not be specifically categorized in any way. Those included resided at the time at New York City, Woodstock, Toronto, Chicago, St. Louis, Minneapolis, Taos, Santa Fe, Laguna Beach, and Carmel-Monterey, among other places. The group includes a number of European artists living at the time in the United States.

the 'atmosphere' be right and that he have material that tends to inspire his best efforts.

II

C spent the first twelve years in a lumber town in Michigan.[1] He had a limited amount of training in professional art schools; believes personality factors, hard work, and persistence to be more important; holds composition to be the fundamental interest of the artist and that all steps in laying out the parts of the picture should be done with greatest care since only through proper placement may the qualities of balance, rhythm, and proportion work to make a picture what it is. The artist discloses his functional efficiency through the degree of aesthetic sensitivity he is able to bring to bear upon a problem.

He believed that finger skill may come from ancestry that had engaged in long periods of fine work. Inheritance is in stock peculiarly adapted to art uses, not directly.

III

U drew at the age of five and related that later in grade school (Louisville, Ky.) boys would fight to sit with him to see his sketches. He worked at lithography and as sketch artist for a Louisville newspaper while studying nights. Later studied in Dresden and at Weimar, Germany. On returning to the United States he attended the Art Institute School at Chicago and still later transferred to a private art school.

U maintains that success in art is largely a matter of bulldogged persistence, with confidence needed to survive reverses. He believes that design is the objective of all art but that nature offers the color and form suggestions.

IV

B was mostly self-taught but attended art school for a period. He interested himself in artistic activities and objects from the age of six, had meager art instruction in the public schools, but most of his serious training came from self-initiated activities and from being around artists in their studios.

---

[1] This painter was one of three who did not demonstrate an *early* activity of some kind of art expression. The interest in his case developed between the ages of twelve and sixteen.

B feels that *organization* is the great objective in art. In practice he picks up ideas here and there and organizes them at the studio into compositions. *B* believes that adherence to strict realism (naturalism) is not desirable, arguing that neither Leonardo da Vinci nor Ghirlandaio was present at the Last Supper to paint it. Some of the best works of art have been conceptions of the artist's imagination—what he was able to reconstruct of a scene now past.

He believed that the canvas should be so organized that it will carry out the emotion of the painter or that the principal element should carry some significant suggestion existing in the picture aside from the objects in it. An immense sky area would hence suggest vastness of expanse; a clear sky area occupying two-thirds or more of the total canvas would suggest the great open spaces of the prairie or plateau country. A good composition should confine itself to a single objective. It may contain many objects (persons, structures, animals), but their lines should be in a definite direction or arranged in unified groupings. (He illustrated his point to the writer in a painting on an easel, centering around a group of Indians at a baseball game, all aligned along a fence with the attention of all toward the left. The heavy mountain mass in the background was painted in unsaturated dull blue with only one gorge developed in a subdued manner.)

The factor of aesthetic sensitivity is of the highest importance. A crudely painted detail such as a bit of sagebrush in the foreground often bothers him until it is integrated more adequately in the picture. He referred to a painting by another artist in the region who was bothered for more than a year by a tree in his picture which had in the end to be entirely repainted.[1]

V

H was born in Indiana and became interested in art at the age of twelve when a billboard scenery painter came to town and *H* "played hooky" two days to watch him. He was interested in

---

[1] The author later visited this same painter and found that he had at the time a canvas under development that had failed to satisfy him. In the author's judgment, the painting should never have been begun since the subject matter was hardly suitable for aesthetic treatment, although this painter was regarded as one of the best technicians of the group.

classic pictures in books, intrigued not by romantic volumes but by Greek art. These stayed with him so well that at the age of forty-six he was able while on a month's visit to his home to remember where certain passages were to the particular part of the page.[1]

Painting should interpret life. Hence, it cannot be a copy of nature—the color camera can beat the best—but it should have living character, balance, proportion, color rhythms, space rhythms, etc. *Space harmony* is the next development in painting, according to *H*. By *space harmony* is meant the relation of each division of the canvas to every other part, considered from every angle. If the area below the horizon is dense, much space must be given to sky; if the ground contains considerable light color, then there may be less sky. The picture should be balanced diagonally as well as up and down, right and left. (Undoubtedly *H* has in mind essentially the same conception understood by others as organic unity. The concept suggests something akin to fourth-dimensional units.)

A picture should have the quality of living nature—not dead statement—and should have rhythm, balance, and proportion, effectively used, so as to carry out some vitalized conception of life. (*Dynamic organization* he regarded as a good expression, but one not carrying the full meaning.) Organization, the significant problem, may be disturbed by even the slightest variation from the proper tone or color. Illustrating from the work of others, *H* stated that Cézanne took the Impressionism of Monet as he found it and added to the featuring of light on color an attempt to get three-dimensional solidity. Likewise, Van Gogh, Gauguin, Seurat, *et al.*, worked on their own variations of what they believed to be important and significant.

VI

G was born in Russia of a Tartar strain, later studied art in France and was badly wounded as a French aviator during the First World War. His art interest goes back to age five; he has notebooks full of early drawings. Some interest was promoted by school, but his father offered much criticism and stimulus.

G regards *vision* (probably synonymous with creative imagination) as greatest factor in art production. It is the conceiving of a situation

---

[1] This, in the author's opinion, is a concrete example of high *perceptual facility* or observational fidelity characteristic of most artists.

as of aesthetic consequence and the execution of it in any way that satisfies the creator of it.

Consistency in purpose is also a great asset to the artist. Once he has the vision he must decide upon the *key* and adhere to it unvaryingly.[1] G related that, at a French art school he attended, each student made a sketch for development. These sketches were placed in a vault for three months, during which time the students worked at their paintings. At the end of the period the sketches were compared with the paintings. Many showed little or no resemblance. Some were in strict accord with the original sketch. This ability to hold to an idea or vision once clearly held is of great importance.

The critical faculty grows, having its full fruition after the age of fifty. Procedures also change. G once followed the practice of outlining his composition; now he paints as soon as he has his conception clearly in mind, beginning with the darkest note. The dominant key always, however, must first, last, and always be kept in mind.

VII

F was born in Russia; his father was a craftsman. He was "always" interested in art. He attended school where art was featured for six years, then spent seven years at state art school, at which he enjoyed a scholarship and later an instructorship.

Most valuable characteristic of artist, F believes, is *individuality.* He must be different; his style should not be commonplace, nor should subjects be ordinary. The canvas should bear the mark of the artist's interpretation of his subject. (F had on the studio wall a small painting of a burro, which, though given glamorous color, was unbelievably expressive of a sleepy, lazy attitude connoting obstinate immovability, particularly pronounced in the drooping head and neck and half-closed eye: it was indeed an 'individual' treatment.)

Next in importance is *technique,* which cannot be overstressed. The artist must know his pigments and brush techniques. He must know what techniques will best develop a given area, what are suitable for this subject or for that.

Mechanical skills are important but not all important. They are more or less necessary, but artists have painted in spite of disabilities. (He mentioned Renoir's inability to hold brush firmly in later years —having it tied to his hand.)

---

[1] *Tonal harmony* is another expression for the quality G described.

Composition is highly important. It determines in advance the probable success or failure of the picture. Every part of the picture must be studied, every line, every color, every color's relationship to every other color—all must be studied exhaustively.

No picture that is worth anything comes by chance. There is no "inspiration." The picture comes only from simple hard work, every part having been studied out as it progresses. If the right start is not made, the artist might as well start all over again.

F does not meticulously outline his composition but merely spots his masses and points of interest, sometimes with the color for that part of the picture. All the color relationships must be worked out from a given tone or beginning, this usually being the dominant mass.

No artist would ever get far without the critical faculty. He must be able to sense faults and weaknesses and detect areas where the composition may be improved.

VIII

P is an American of English-Italian extraction. Painted at early age.

He holds that art principles make art what it is. There are fundamental qualities in good art that will be sensed by the public. The artist feels them subconsciously. If the picture does not appeal to the public it is usually the artist who is at fault: he has failed to get his message across.

The good picture will have discernible rhythms, color balance, satisfying color relationships, as in color highlights, reflections, shadows, etc. There will be an easy flow from line to line, color note to color note. (In painting one of his best pictures he failed to get anything at first save a static, lifeless composition. After spending some time exploring he observed four Indian girls in poses that fitted the need of the composition and sketched them on the spot. Then details were changed to enhance certain rhythms, with color suggestions from a studio rug for enrichment and greater approximation of unity.)

IX

S is of Scotch-Irish descent. He has vigorous, forceful character. His father was a cabinetmaker. Craftsman propensity was in evidence in early childhood; he literally 'devoured' books on mechanics and the making of small articles; drawing activities came into prominence at age of seven. He 'illustrated' *Treasure Island* on blank pages at end of chapters at seventeen.

He believes in utilizing subject matter depicting the everyday living of everyday folk. The work in each case, however, should follow the standards of good composition and technical excellence. He believes contemporary artists may profit from study of methods and techniques of medieval masters, and was currently experimenting with initial use of tempera directly on canvas, followed by varnish, over which was used transparent oil colors.

He believed that the craftsman attitude is highly important, and once argued with fellow jurymen to give a first award to an obscure painter who had a simple composition well painted. He holds that change of scene is desirable to prevent artist's growing stale and staying too long with overworked subject matter.

X

C is a woman. She painted at early age and produced for author's inspection excellent compositions in water color made at age of eight. She is now classified as progressive type, tending toward abstract painting or semiabstract, using figures and objects in deep space. Regards abstract form as the artist's conception of his subject matter. Assumes no painter can really see the materials before him as they are and that no two persons are capable of seeing the same object in the same way. Hence, it is argued, what is organized is a pattern of relationships and a unity that the artist must develop in the light of his own experience and knowledge.

Holds that 'fourth-dimensional' painting offers the challenge to the serious, thinking, modern painter. The fourth-dimensional aspect exists in the creation of a pervasive atmosphere. The usual three dimensions take care of the illusion of space (depth), but the diagonal (fourth-dimension) quality is attained either by special handling of the material or by a pervasive tonal quality more or less separated from the usual atmospheric haze (aerial perspective).

Fourth-dimensional painting moreover implies a single viewpoint that remains constant from any angle, and the objects in the composition remain in their respective positions no matter what the viewpoint of the spectator is. Models are never employed, and all human forms are treated semiabstractly. (A painting then in studio labeled "Primitive Mother" was an abstract conception of a cliff dweller's habitat, developed from related sense data plus research, this procedure being necessary since no living person has ever seen the cliff dwellers.)

XI

W's interest was demonstrated at early age: craftsman—jewelry worker, leather worker, cabinetmaker. He is an artist of superior intelligence, consistent drive, and deep interest in the role of art in present-day society. His painting has progressed through several stages; now his tendency is toward clean-cut stylized treatment, with exceptional clarity of color and simplification of form.

He believes best art is produced by assiduous study of thematic material, such study preceding the actual sketch of the picture plan. The themes should have relation to the known interests of society. The treatment of the theme requires diligent study. Resort to line arrangements as a kind of scaffolding may result in better allover organization and effective unity, which is also furthered by simplifying the palette. *W* follows the plan of working out the final sketch before painting in complete and meticulous detail in order better to develop the composition and, more important, to arrive at a satisfactory working out of light-and-dark values. The activity of *W* is not confined by traditional methods and practices. Many thinly painted layers of pigment interspersed by careful glazing are sometimes employed to produce the desired texture or to effect some particular quality. Resort to thin-lead colored pencils has also been used for particular objectives in drawings, and the same meticulous care has featured his lithographs.

Although not often directly employing the terms, *W* has amply demonstrated his valuation of qualities such as balance, rhythm, harmony, and unity. Like many able painters and true artists he has taken them for granted and concentrated on the creation of subject matter that has had great human interest and wide appeal.

XII

P is of Armenian extraction and an individual of tremendous nervous energy and drive, one of the greatest artists of modern times. He is Paris trained, widely traveled, and an inveterate collector of *objets d'art*. He has unerring sense of finely composed aesthetic values and is a master of technical exactitude.

He regards composition as largely a matter of fitting together congruous and harmonious elements in such a manner that the unity is unmistakable. Unity embraces fine adjustment of all values: line, mass, color, light-dark, and intricate interrelationships of all elements in the composition.

Holds that the artist cannot advance without at least three qualities: mastery of technical proficiency (which probably all good artists have), extensive knowledge of the chemistry and handling of pigments (which, he stated some artists, notably Whistler, did not have), and unerring sensitivity to formal values, as residing in effective balance, rhythm, and all qualities contributing toward the attainment of unity and harmony.

XIII

B sketched and drew at early age. He is an avid student of people, particularly in out-of-the-way localities, and of metropolitan life as well. Widely traveled in the United States, he possesses rich "sketch notations" of Americana. He takes art as a serious occupation requiring intelligence, industry, and planning as much as professions such as law or medicine.

He assumes there are definite suggestions to be had from artists of any period, but the individual's own manner should in the end prevail. He disdains simple representation and reconstructs his original material with studied distortion to express qualities he wants them to have in the light of the needs of his composition. His compositions are frequently planned as though the characters and surroundings (properties) occupied positions on a stage. In this way the effect of deep space, balance spatially, and certain rhythms are effected. The same dynamic unity seen in some of Renoir's organizations is obtained but in a different style and with a quite different technique.

The philosophy of art held by *B* embraces the belief that art should interpret life honestly, searchingly, and without reservation. To him it is an instance of telling the truth, the whole truth, and nothing but the truth—as, of course, he sees it. And to get at the truth he is unsparing in his efforts to dig down into musty records, "old-timer's" stories, photographs, newspaper material, histories, and whatever source is available to get the necessary data. Here in truth is an artist who actually indulges in *research* in a real sense and brings to art a competence and sincerity that are unusual. In this respect he is essentially a scholar with the true research spirit.

The plan followed by *B* of working out all essential aspects of his composition in gross forms, often also in clay, inevitably assures him of a composition in which every part is working—contributing something toward the total unity in a direct, forceful manner. The figures seem to revolve about a spatially central pivot point, this being effected largely by attitudinal positioning and placement. The figures appear furthermore to be woven into the setting so that even the surrounding and accessories appear to contribute to a dynamic, living quality, reminiscent somewhat of the swirling, twisting qualities found in Van Gogh's later landscapes, suggesting growth processes, and the dynamism of El Greco.

B is typical of the contemporary American artist who stands on his own feet, observant of and familiar with traditional practices, but who has the high intelligence and personality traits to guide an independently developed manner of his own. With technical ability comparable to the best, he applies it to original objectives and subject matter of his own conceiving. To his credit should go a further restatement of the functions of art to include interpretation of life wherever found, and the tenet that art even in touching upon "forgotten" areas and peoples can be made dynamic, significant, and permanently vital in the affairs of man.

XIV

P is of Hungarian origin, versatile, resourceful, dynamic, and competent in such widely diversified activities as mural painting, color illustration, and etching.

He believes great works can be achieved by assiduous study and arduous work. The studio is essentially a workshop. [His had a library (source material) and a grand piano, yet permitted occasions alternating between informal social activities and periods of intense application to the project in hand.]

Nothing is left to guess or to "free imagination." The contemplation and planning of a mural is always preceded by intensive study of the objectives, the possible ways of expressing the theme, the forms (and of course economy of forms) through which the theme may be expressed, and the practical steps in carrying out the whole project. Details such as the appropriate color theme, expressiveness of a particular color key, and the utilization of color notes are not overlooked.

XV

H. German, now residing in America. Comes from line that dates back to early seventeenth century with some members engaged in craftsman activities in nearly every generation.

H believes art should serve humanity rather than confine itself to a search for abstract beauty. The artist should have his studio in the teeming centers and the places where human experience and emotions show themselves. In another sense a function of art should mirror man and his follies as well as his virtues. War, social injustice, the inadequacy of institutions and other aspects of maladjustment in society may forcefully be presented.[1] Subject matter of social import becomes art when it is aesthetically treated. Hence each conception needs to be given study for the purpose of translating actual realities into symbolic and abstract or semiabstract forms, these to be fitted into a composition aesthetically organized. *H* features unusual coloring, designed to make the significant element stand out and to convey expressive qualities that further the complete understanding of the idea.

Philosophic conceptions, religious truths, human aspiration— these may also form the basic theme of an artist's conception. New methods should be the constant concern of the alert and creative artist. It is wholly unnecessary to follow traditional ways of presenting a theme nor is it desirable that artists confine their interests to hackneyed subject matter and trite aspects of life. The masses may be the inspiration and also the aspiration of mankind to realize deeper understanding of life, greater spiritual values, and more tangible aspects of social justice.

---

[1] This need not cause any reader to exclaim: "Ah—he wants the artist to be a propagandist." Propaganda is a systematic, continued attempt to influence others by control over the stimuli affecting them. An occasional painting expressing the savagery of man in war, or the pitiful faces, depressed attitudinal bearing, and environment of old men discarded by industry is not propaganda unless it is a part of a series, unless it forms a link in a systematically presented drive to effect an ulterior end.

The fifteen artists whose manner of work, individual philosophy, and ideas on creative process have been presented by no means exhaust the range of artist types. Although no doubt there are scores of artists similar to each of these, there are still different types, such as those of complex character like Picasso and men who are highly regarded for a single phase of portrait painting. The class of extreme abstractionists are also absent, but these, it may be said, represent a small minority. For the most part, the fifteen selected were chosen as being representative of a variety of interests and because they were available for direct study. It is believed that the artist himself can supply under suitable circumstances more insight into creative processes than can be derived from other less direct sources. The material should at least clarify some of the vague notions surrounding creative processes of the artist.

INDEX

❧❦❧